英訳付き

ニッポンの名前図鑑
日本建築・生活道具

監修　山本成一郎

An Illustrated Guide to
Japanese Traditional Architecture
and Everyday Things

Editorial Supervisor　Yamamoto Seiichiro

淡交社

はじめに

茶室で見られる「アノ」小さい出入り口は、なんていう名前？
「葛籠」って、どんなもの？
どうやって「床の間」を英語で説明したらいい？

日本に暮らしていても、意外に知らない事物が身の回りに多く
あります。形を知っていても、名前がわからないモノ。名前を
聞いても、どんな形か想像できないモノ。名前と形を知ってい
ても、具体的に由来やいわれを説明できないモノ。さらに、それ
を英語で説明するなんて……。
近年では、「Tatami」や「Washi」といった日本語が外国の方にも
通じたり、英語辞書の中に収録されるほど一般的になっていま
す。また、外国人旅行者が畳での生活を体験したり、日本の寺社
仏閣を観に行くこともあります。和の文化が世界的に注目され
ているにも関わらず、日本の事物を日本語でも英語でも説明で
きないのは、日本人にとって心もとないことです。
本書では、伝統的な「日本建築」「生活道具」にまつわるモノの
名前を取り上げました。日本人として知っておきたい代表的な
名前を選び、和名・英名、和名のローマ字表記を掲載し、いわれ
などの詳細まで付しました。ただし、モノの名前には地域性が
あり、本書で紹介するものがすべての地域に対応するわけでは
ないことをご了承ください。
これまで目をつぶってきた日本特有のモノを見つめ直しましょ
う。友人や外国の方にさらっと説明ができると、少し誇らしく
ありませんか？

Introduction

What is that small entrance to a tea room called?
What exactly is a *tuzura*?
And how can I explain *tokonoma* in English?

Living in Japan, we find that there are many things around us we don't know. Things we know what they look like, but cannot remember their names. Things we cannot imagine what they look like even when we hear their names. And things for which we know the names, but cannot explain their origins. When we can't explain to others what they are in Japanese, how could we in English?

Recently, Japanese terms such as tatami or *washi* are understood by foreign people and such words can be found in English language dictionaries. It has become popular for visitors to Japan to experience living in tatami rooms or to visit temples and shrines. Japanese culture is attracting attention around the globe. In such situations, it is somewhat sad if a Japanese person cannot explain his or her own culture in Japanese nor in English.

In this book, we have picked up things related to traditional Japanese architecture and everyday life. They are all things that one, as a Japanese would want to know. For each item, its Japanese name, English name and pronunciation are put together with an explanation. However, please note that names differ among regions and that the names used in this book may not be common in some regions.

Now, let's reexamine the things that we have overlooked in our country. Wouldn't it be wonderful if you could explain these things to your friends and to people all over the world?

CONTENTS

日本建築
JAPANESE TRADITIONAL ARCHITECTURE

京町家　Machiya townhouses in Kyoto

犬矢来・inuyarai	12
虫籠窓・mushiko-mado　羽目板張り・hameita-bari	
腰壁・koshi-kabe／腰板壁・koshi-ita-kabe	13
通り庭・tori-niwa／ハシリ・hashiri	
舞良戸・mairado　暖簾・noren	15
坪庭・tsubo-niwa	16
縁側・engawa　簾・sudare	
沓脱石・kutsunugi-ishi／踏石・fumi-ishi	17

瓦葺き住宅　Tile-roofed houses

大棟・omune　降棟・kudarimune	18
鬼瓦・oni-gawara　平側・hira-gawa	
妻・tsuma／妻側・tsuma-gawa	19

屋根　Roofs

切妻造り・kirizuma-zukuri	
入母屋造り・irimoya-zukuri　寄棟造り・yosemune-zukuri	20
宝形（方形）造り・hogyo-zukuri	
片流れ・katanagare　招き造り・maneki-zukuri	21

茅葺き民家　Thatched houses

茅葺き屋根・kayabuki-yane　破風・hafu	22
式台玄関・shikidai-genkan　大戸口・otoguchi　戸袋・tobukuro	23
土間・doma／三和土・tataki	
竈・kudo (kamado)／へっつい・hettsui　釜・kama	25
囲炉裏・irori　自在鉤・jizai-kagi　小猿鉤・kozaru-kagi	27

近代住宅　Modern houses

| 長屋・nagaya | 28 |
| 文化住宅・bunka-jutaku | 29 |

座敷　Tatami rooms

畳・tatami　欄間・ramma	31
鞘の間・saya-no-ma　鴨居・kamoi	
敷居・shiki-i　長押・nageshi	33
床の間・toko-no-ma／床・toko	34
脇床・waki-doko／床脇・toko-waki　違い棚・chigai-dana	
天袋・ten-bukuro／袋戸棚・fukuro-todana	
付書院・tsuke-shoin／出書院・de-shoin	35

建具　Sliding doors

| 襖・fusuma | 36 |
| 障子・shoji | 37 |

窓　Windows

武者窓・musha-mado　与力窓・yoriki-mado	
下地窓・shitaji-mado／塗り残し窓・nurinokoshi-mado	38
格子窓・koshi-mado／出格子・degoshi	
連子窓・renji-mado　火灯（花頭）窓・kato-mado	39

天井　Ceilings

| 格天井・gou-tenjo　鏡天井・kagami-tenjo | 40 |
| 折上天井・oriage-tenjo　棹縁天井・saobuchi-tenjo | 41 |

風呂　Baths

銭湯・sento　ペンキ絵・penkie	42
風呂桶・furo-oke　片手桶・katate-oke	43
檜風呂・hinoki-buro　五右衛門風呂・goemon-buro	44
露天風呂・roten-buro／野天風呂・noten-buro	45

茶室　Tea huts

躙口・nijiri-guchi　土間庇・doma-bisashi　扁額・hengaku	47
点前座・temae-za	48
炉畳・ro-datami　給仕口・kyuji-guchi／火灯口・kato-guchi	
腰張・koshi-bari	
掛込天井・kakekomi-tenjo／化粧屋根裏・kesho-yane-ura	49

露地　Tea hut gardens

| 蹲踞・tsukubai | 50 |

飛石・tobi-ishi　枝折戸・shiorido
関守石・sekimori-ishi／留め石・tome-ishi　　　　51

石灯籠　Stone lanterns
春日灯籠・kasuga-doro　雪見灯籠・yukimi-doro　　52
琴柱（徽軫）灯籠・kotoji-doro　塔灯篭・to-doro　　53

垣根　Fences
四つ目垣・yotsume-gaki　萩垣・hagi-gaki　　54
建仁寺垣・kenninji-gaki　矢来垣・yarai-gaki　　55

日本庭園　Japanese gardens
浄土式庭園・jodoshiki-teien　　56
池泉回遊式庭園・chisen-kaiyushiki-teien　　57
三尊石・sanzonseki　　58
沢渡石・sawatari-ishi　　59
砂盛・sunamori　　60
枯山水庭園・karesansui-teien　砂紋・samon　　61
［砂紋の種類］　青海波紋・seigaiha-mon　流水紋・ryusui-mon　62
　　　　　　　水紋・sui-mon　荒波紋・aranami-mon　63

城　Castles
天守・tenshu　　64
櫓・yagura　鯱・shachihoko (shachi)　　65

神社　Shrines
神明鳥居・shimmei-torii　　66
明神鳥居・myojin-torii　　67
大社造り・taisha-zukuri　　68
神明造り・shimmei-zukuri　　69
流造り・nagare-zukuri　　70
水盤舎・suibansha／手水舎・chozuya　柄杓・hishaku　71
賽銭箱・saisen-bako　狛犬・komainu／獅子・shishi　72
注連縄・shime-nawa　紙垂（四手）・shide　73
鈴・suzu　　74
おみくじ・omikuji　　75

寺院　Temples
四脚門・shikyaku-mon　　76
楼門・ro-mon　仁王像・niozo　　77
仏殿・butsuden　懸魚・gegyo　鳥衾・toribusuma　78
向拝柱・kohai-bashira　　79

五重塔・goju-no-to　相輪・sorin
風鐸・futaku／宝鐸・hotaku (hochaku)　　　　81

生活道具
JAPANESE TRADITIONAL EVERYDAY THINGS

家具　Furniture

桐簞笥・kiri-tansu　　　　　　　　　　　　84

階段簞笥・kaidan-tansu／箱簞笥・hako-tansu　　85

飾り棚・kazari-dana　衣桁・iko　　　　　　　86

鏡台・kyo-dai　姿見・sugatami　　　　　　　87

卓袱台・chabu-dai　座卓・zataku　　　　　　88

座布団・zabuton　座椅子・zaisu　脇息・kyosoku　89

関東火鉢・kanto-hibachi／長火鉢・naga-hibachi／

手焙り・te-aburi　　　　　　　　　　　　　90

蚊帳・kaya　　　　　　　　　　　　　　　91

蚊取り線香・katori-senko／蚊遣り線香・kayari-senko

蚊取り豚・katori-buta／蚊遣り豚・kayari-buta　92

葛籠・tsuzura　行李・kori　　　　　　　　　93

長持・nagamochi

乱箱・midare-bako／乱衣装箱・midare-isho-bako　94

衝立・tsuitate　　　　　　　　　　　　　　95

屏風・byobu　　　　　　　　　　　　　　　96

勝手屏風・katte-byobu／水屋屏風・mizuya-byobu　97

掛物・kakemono／掛け軸・kakejiku　自在・jizai　99

灯火具　Lamps

足元行灯・ashimoto-andon　　　　　　　　　100

短檠・tankei　手燭・teshoku　　　　　　　　101

提灯・chochin　盆提灯・bon-chochin

祭り提灯・matsuri-chochin　　　　　　　　　102

馬乗提灯・umanori-chochin　小田原提灯・odawara-chochin　103

目次

文房具　Stationery

筆・fude／毛筆・mohitsu　104

筆架・hikka　墨・sumi　硯・suzuri　硯屏・kembyo　105

水滴・suiteki　文鎮・bunchin　106

印章・insho／印鑑・inkan　印泥・indei／印肉・in-niku　107

和紙・washi　108

奉書紙・hoshoshi　檀紙・danshi　半紙・hanshi　109

千代紙・chiyogami　110

折り紙・origami　111

短冊・tanzaku　色紙・shikishi　巻子・kansu　112

和綴じ本・watoji-bon／和装本・waso-bon／和帳・wacho

折本・ori-hon　113

美術品の箱　Boxes for art

箱書・hako-gaki／書付・kakitsuke

真田紐・sanada-himo　四方掛け結び・yoho-kake-musubi　115

桟蓋・sambuta　落款・rakkan／落成款識・rakuseikanshi　117

香道具　Utensils for incense ceremonies

香木・kouboku　練香・nerikou　118

香炉・kouro／聞香炉・kiki-kouro　銀葉・gin-yo　119

炭団・tadon／香炭団・kou-tadon　折据・orisue　120

銀葉盤・gin-yo-ban

源氏香之図・genjiko-no-zu／源氏香・genjiko　121

贈答　Gifts

祝儀袋・shugi-bukuro　不祝儀袋・bu-shugi-bukuro　122

熨斗・noshi／折り熨斗・ori-noshi／熨斗鮑・noshi-awabi

熨斗紙・noshi-gami／掛け紙・kake-gami　123

水引・mizuhiki　真結び・ma-musubi／結び切り・musubi-kiri

両輪結び・morowana-musubi　124

鮑結び・awabi-musubi／淡路結び・awaji-musubi

鮑返し・awabi-gaeshi／淡路返し・awaji-gaeshi　125

大入袋・oiri-bukuro　ポチ袋・pochi-bukuro　126

袱紗・fukusa　切手盆・kittebon　127

神棚　Shinto family altars

宮形・miyagata　御神札（御札）・ofuda　128

神鏡・shinkyo　榊・sakaki　瓶子・heishi

平瓮・hiraka　水玉・mizutama／水器・suiki　129

仏壇　Buddhist family altars

| 仏壇・butsudan　本尊・honzon　位牌・ihai | 131 |

墓　Graves

棹石・sao-ishi／仏石・hotoke-ishi
香炉（墓前用）・kouro　　　　　　　　　　　　　　132
墓誌・boshi　納骨室・nokotsushitsu／カロート・karoto
卒塔婆・sotoba　　　　　　　　　　　　　　　　　133

畳のサイズ　The size of tatami mats　　　　　　　82
索引（五十音順）　Index for Japanese　　　　　　134

本書の英訳について

1. モノ・コトの名前には、読み方（ヘボン式ローマ字表記）と英語名を掲載していま
   す。基本的にモノ・コトの名前の読み方はヘボン式ローマ字で表記していますが、
   香道具（118-121頁）においてのみ、「香（こう）」をkouと表記しています。
2. 英語名は必ずしも定型表現ではありません。
3. 英訳文の中で、日本語読みのまま使用していることばは、イタリック（斜体）表記
   にしていますが、Oxford Advanced Learner's Dictionary 9th editionに英語として
   登録されていることばは正体にしています。
4. 日本語の説明文と、英語の説明文とが対応していない場合（英訳では解説を割愛
   した箇所）があります。

About the Translation

1. The pronunciation of Japanese words in this book is written in the Hepburn Romanization
   system. However, the term *kou* used in pages 118 to 121 is an exception.
2. Please note that the English names may not necessarily be a fixed translation.
3. Japanese words are shown in italics, except those in the Oxford Advanced Learner's
   Dictionary 9th Edition, which are in normal font.
4. In some parts, explanations have been omitted in the course of translating from Japanese
   to English.

日本建築

JAPANESE TRADITIONAL ARCHITECTURE

京町家

町家（まちや／ちょうか）とは昔の町人や商人の家。間口が狭く、奥行きがある京都市街の町家は「京町家」とも呼ばれ、現在も住居、カフェ、レストラン、宿泊所として利用されている。

外観

The exterior of *machiya* in Kyoto

格子窓・*koshi-mado*／
出格子・*degoshi*

→p. 39

犬矢来・*inuyarai*

Protective screen

軒下の壁際に置かれる囲いのこと。人や馬などが家を傷つけないようにするための建具だが、現在では景観にも一役買っている。

Inuyarai are curved bamboo fences that are placed under the eaves and cover the lower part of the outer walls. They were originally put up to form a boundary between the road and the *machiya* to protect the house from getting damaged from passersby or horses.

Machiya townhouses in Kyoto

Machiya, also known as *chouka*, are traditional townhouses of merchants. *Machiya* in Kyoto which have narrow frontages and extend far back from the streets are called *Kyo-machiya*. Today, they are used not only as houses but also as cafes, restaurants and accommodations.

1

虫籠窓 · *mushiko-mado*

Finely latticed window

二階の窓格子を土と漆喰（しっくい）で塗り込めたもの。採光と風通し、防火の役割を果たす。名前の由来は諸説あるが、虫籠（むしかご／むしこ）の形に似ているためとされる。

Mushiko-mado, which literally means "insect cage-like windows," are plastered earthen lattice windows on the second floor of *machiya* houses. These windows provide sunlight and air to the house and work as a means of fire prevention. Among other etymologies, one comes from its shape which resembles an insect cage.

2

羽目板張り · *hameita-bari*

Boarded wall

板を平らに並べて張ったものを「羽目」、その板を「羽目板」という。

Hameita-bari is a type of board wall. When the boards are put up flat, side by side, this state is called *hame*, and the boards which are used are called *hame-ita*.

3

腰壁 · *koshi-kabe* ／腰板壁 · *koshi-ita-kabe*

Wainscoting

「腰」は建築用語で壁の低い部分を指す。壁の低い部分（腰壁）を板張りにしたものを「腰板壁」という。

Koshi, meaning waist, is an architectural terminology which indicates the lower part of a wall. When the lower part of a wall is boarded up waist-high, this is called *koshi-kabe*, literally meaning "waist wall."

京町家

Machiya townhouses in Kyoto

日本建築

通り庭・*tori-niwa*／ハシリ・*hashiri*
Open corridor

表の出入り口から裏口へ通り抜けできる土間。入り口付近は店舗、奥は台所の機能を持ち、「走り庭」「ハシリ」とも呼ばれる。建物上部には天窓付きの吹き抜けがあり、採光と換気、室温調節の役割を果たす。「ハシリ」の由来は、その家の主婦が走るように立ち働くことから。

A *tori-niwa* is an earthen-floored corridor that leads from the front to the rear entrance of the house. The area near the entrance is used as a storefront, and the back, which is called *hashiri-niwa* or *hashiri*, is used as a kitchen. These spaces have double-height ceilings with skylights which provide light, serve as ventilation and control room temperature.

____ 1
舞良戸・*mairado*
Wooden door with horizontal slats

引き違いの板戸を「遣戸（やりど）」といい、そのうち、表側に「舞良子（まいらこ）」と呼ばれる桟を細かく取り付けたものを舞良戸という。

Double sliding doors are called *yarido* in Japanese. When thin strips of wood called *mairako* are attached horizontally to the front side of the doors, they are called *mairado*.

____ 2
暖簾・*noren*
Curtain

商店が店先に掲げる布、もしくは部屋の仕切りとなる布のこと。縄や竹でつくられることもある。商店の暖簾（のれん）には屋号などが描かれており、店の信用や格式を表す。そこに勤めた人が、同じ屋号を使って自らの店舗を構えるのが許されることを「暖簾分け」という。

Noren is a type of curtain generally made from cloth. They are hung between rooms as partitions or at storefronts. They are sometimes made from ropes and bamboo. *Noren* hung at storefronts bear the name and trademark of a shop to symbolize its reputation and standing.

蹲踞 ·
tsukubai
→ p. 50

石灯籠 ·
ishi-doro
→ p. 52

坪庭 · *tsubo-niwa*

Pocket garden

屋内に設けられた、小さな庭のこと。ささやかな植物と蹲踞（50頁）、石
灯籠（52頁）などで構成される。奥行きがあって薄暗い町家に風光を取
り込む機能もある。

A *tsubo-niwa* is a small garden inside the house which consists of plants, a
washbasin set (page 50), stone lanterns (page 52), etc. This garden provides
light and air to the dark and narrow *machiya*.

—— 1

縁側・*engawa*
Veranda

建物の縁（へり）に張り出して設けられた板敷きの部分。座敷と外を繋ぐ出入り口にもなる。縁が建物の外にある場合を「外縁」「濡れ縁」、内側にある場合を「内縁」という。

An *engawa* is a board-floored area projecting from the perimeter of the house. It also serves as an entrance which leads directly to the room.

—— 2

簾・*sudare*
Blinds

細い割り竹や葦（あし）を何本も並べて糸で編み繋いだものが「簾（す）」で、軒（のき）に吊り下げられたものを「簾（すだれ）」という。「御簾（みす）」は、座敷で間仕切りとして使用される縁付きのもの。

Su refers to thin bamboo sticks or reeds woven together with thread. When they are hung under the eaves, they are called a *sudare*. *Misu* specifically refers to *sudare* with hems that are used as room partitions.

—— 3

沓脱石・*kutsunugi-ishi*／踏石・*fumi-ishi*
Shoe-removing stone

玄関や縁側など、出入り口に置かれた石。部屋の内に入る際、この上で履き物を脱ぐ。

A *kutsunugi-ishi* is a stone placed at the entrance or in front of the *engawa* as a place where one steps to remove one's shoes.

瓦葺き住宅

瓦は粘土を成型して焼いた屋根専用部材。神社や寺院に用いられていた瓦は、江戸時代の終わり頃から明治にかけて、板や茅葺きだった一般住宅にも使われ始めたとされる。

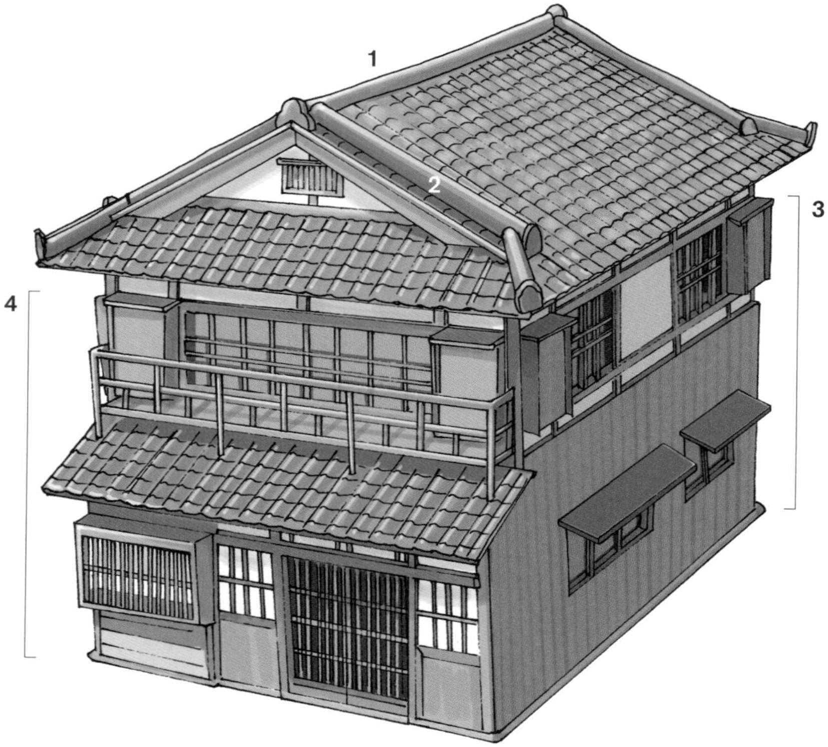

1

大棟・*omune*

Main ridge

屋根の一番高い水平の部分を「大棟」という。

Ridges are called *mune* and the topmost horizontal ridge is specifically referred to as *omune*.

2

降棟・*kudarimune*

Descending ridge

大棟から屋根の流れに沿って降る部分。入母屋造り（20頁）などに見られる。

Ridges that descend from the main ridge are called *kudarimune*. They can be seen on combination roofs (page 20).

Kawara are roof tiles made of clay. *Kawara* tiles were used for shrines and temples up until the Edo period. Then, from the end of the Edo period to the Meiji period, these tiles spread to use in normal houses where wooden and thatched roofs were more popular.

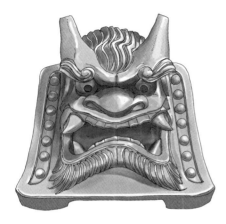

鬼瓦 · *oni-gawara*
Ridge-end tile

屋根の大棟や降棟の端を飾る瓦のこと。鬼の顔を表しているが、蓮華文など他の意匠の場合もある。家に邪悪なものが入ってこないための魔除けを意味する。

Oni-gawara is a type of ornamental *kawara* used to decorate the ends of roof ridges. The most popular ones come in forms of demons, but some other common ones include lotus flower shapes. They ward off evil spirits from haunting the house.

瓦葺き住宅　Tile-roofed houses

3
平側 · *hira-gawa*
Exterior wall

屋根の大棟に並行する面のこと。

Hira-gawa is the outer wall that is parallel to the main ridge.

4
妻 · *tsuma* ／妻側 · *tsuma-gawa*
Gable end wall

屋根の平側と90度をなす面。大棟の両側の屋根端が三角形をつくる。

Tsuma are the triangle-shaped outer walls that are at right angles with the exterior wall.

日本建築

屋根

日本の伝統的な建築には瓦や茅などさまざまな素材を使った屋根が見られるが、屋根の形も多種多様である。ここでは、その一部を紹介する。

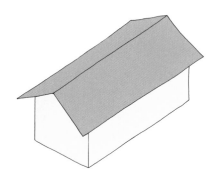

切妻造り
- *kirizuma-zukuri*

Gabled roof

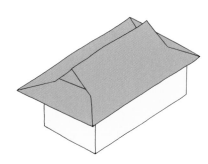

入母屋造り
- *irimoya-zukuri*

Combination roof

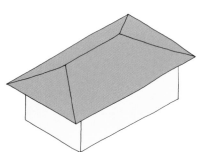

寄棟造り
- *yosemune-zukuri*

Hip roof

Roofs

The roofs of traditional Japanese architecture come in various types such as tiled and thatched. Their forms also vary. Here are a few examples.

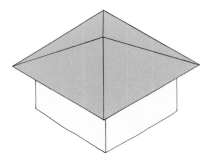

宝形（方形）造り
・ *hogyo-zukuri*
Square pyramidal roof

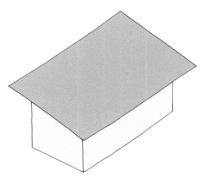

片流れ
・ *katanagare*
Shed roof

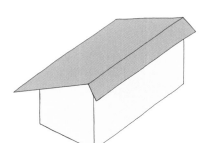

招き造り
・ *maneki-zukuri*
Saltbox roof

農村で収穫される茅や藁（わら）で屋根を葺いた民家。地方の風土によって、曲家（まがりや）、合掌造りなど形はさまざまだが、一部を除き、現在住居として使われている茅葺き民家は少ない。

外観

The exterior of thatched houses

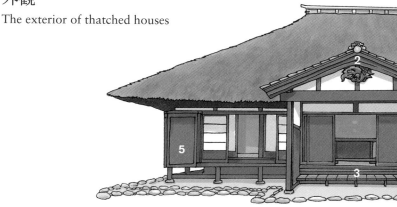

1

茅葺き屋根 · *kayabuki-yane*

Thatched roofs

稲藁（いなわら）、麦藁、葦（あし）、薄（すすき）など、屋根を葺くイネ科の植物を総称して「茅」と呼ぶ。藁の場合は「藁葺き」ということもある。雨風にさらされて傷むと葺き替える必要があるが、現在は大量の茅がとれないため保存が難しい。

Kaya is a general term which refers to plants in the Gramineae family that are used to thatch roofs. Straw from rice and wheat, reeds and Japanese pampas grass are included in this category.

2

破風 · *hafu*

Roof gable

妻側（19頁）の三角形の部分、もしくはそこに取り付けられた板を「破風（はふ）」という。「唐破風」や「千鳥破風」などの種類がある。

Hafu refers to the triangular shape at the gable end wall (page 19), or to the board attached to the roof gable.

Thatched houses

These ordinary folk-houses have thatched roofs made with materials such as straw from crops harvested in the farming villages. Japan has many different types of houses with thatched roofs, depending on each region's climate. However today, not many thatched houses are used for housing.

式台玄関 · *shikidai-genkan*

Entrance for guests

客人や身分の高い人を迎え入れるために、板敷きにした玄関。

A *shikidai-genkan* is an entrance with a wooden floor set at a slightly lower level than the rooms to welcome in guests or people of high birth.

大戸口 · *otoguchi*

Entrance for the family

家人が日常的に出入りするところ。

An *otoguchi* is an entrance used daily by the inhabitants.

戸袋 · *tobukuro*

Shutter box

建物の一番外側に建てる戸「雨戸」を収納しておくための箱状の設備。縁側や窓の敷居の端に取り付ける。

Tobukuro are box-like structures for storing storm shutters, which are the outermost doors of a house. They are attached to the veranda or the ends of windowsills.

土間・*doma* ／三和土・*tataki*
Earth or mortar floored area

屋内で床を張らずに地面のまま、もしくは土や漆喰で仕上げた空間。土間のうち、土に石灰やにがりなどを混ぜて叩き固めたものを「三和土（たたき）」といい、農家によく見られ、玄関、台所、生産作業の場、集会所など多様な役割を果たす。

A *doma* is a space inside the house without floorboards but with earthen floors or plastered floors. When the floor of *doma* is made by blending lime and bittern with soil, it is called *tataki*. This space is often seen in farm houses and can serve as an entrance, a kitchen, a workplace, a place for gathering, etc.

1

竈・*kudo (kamado)* ／へっつい・*hettsui*
Cooking stove

鍋釜を火にかけて煮炊きするためのコンロで、土間に築かれる。下に焚き口が設けられ、投入する薪（まき／たきぎ）や炭の量で火加減する。

A *kudo* is a cooking stove built in a *doma*. It has a place for putting fire-wood and charcoal. The fire needs to be managed with the amount of fuel.

2

釜・*kama*
Cooker

米を炊いたり、湯を沸かしたりする鉄製の道具。周囲に羽がついており、竈（くど／かまど）に引っ掛けて、釜の底部分を加熱する。

A *kama* is an iron pot used for cooking rice or boiling water. It has a brim to put it over fire in a *kudo*.

居間
Sitting room

1

囲炉裏 ・ *irori*
Fireside

床を四角にくり抜いて、灰や炭を入れ、火を熾（おこ）すようにした場所。暖房や煮炊きに使用する。ダイニングルームと同じ役割で、囲炉裏を囲みながら食事やお茶を楽しんだ。

An *irori* is a square pit set flush with the floor where ashes and charcoal are put for making fire. It was used for heating and cooking and it served as today's dining room. People gathered around the *irori* to enjoy meals and tea.

2

自在鉤 ・ *jizai-kagi*
Pot hook

囲炉裏や炉の火の上に、鍋や鉄瓶を吊るすための装置。高さを自由自在に調整できるところからのネーミング。自在鉤の上部に格子組みの棚がつけられていることがあり、そこに衣類や食べ物を吊るして乾燥させる。

A *jizai-kagi* is a hook used for hanging pots and iron kettles over the fire at an *irori* or over a hearth. In some houses, this pot hook is attached to a wooden lattice rack or panel which is suspended from the rafters. This rack is used for drying clothes and food.

3

小猿鉤 ・ *kozaru-kagi*
Wooden friction stopper

自在鉤の高さを調節するための横木のこと。

A *kozaru-kagi* is a piece of wood used for adjusting the height of the pot hook.

長屋・*nagaya*
Row house

江戸時代からつづく形式。江戸時代の長屋は一棟の家を、数戸に分割し
た賃貸住居。台所は土間で、風呂はない。住人は井戸、トイレ、ごみ捨て
場を共同で使用した。現在では、複数の戸建てを横長に並べた集合住宅
をいい、1階建て、2階建てなどさまざまな形式がある。

Nagaya, literally "long house," is a type of housing from the Edo period
onward. In the Edo period, one house was split into several dwellings for
rent. Different inhabitants shared a well, a toilet, and the garbage dump.
Although each household had their own earthen kitchens, there were no
baths in these row houses. They can be either one or two stories high.

Among various types of housings from the Meiji period to the Showa period, here are two representative housings characteristic to Japan.

文化住宅・*bunka-jutaku*
Semi-Western style house

大正時代から昭和時代にかけて流行した和洋折衷の住宅を指す。応接室や玄関に洋風が取り入れられた。一方で、関西では木造2階建ての集合住宅を「文化住宅」と呼ぶこともある。

Bunka-jutaku refers to a type of half-Japanese half-Western style housing that was popular from the Taisho period to the Showa period. Its drawing rooms and entrances were Western style. In the Kansai region of Japan, wooden two-story apartments are sometimes called *bunka-jutaku*.

座敷

室町時代以前の住居は板の間が基本だったが、書院造りの流行とともに畳を敷き詰めた座敷が一般的になっていった。また、現在の和室を特徴付ける「床の間」（34頁）も発達した。

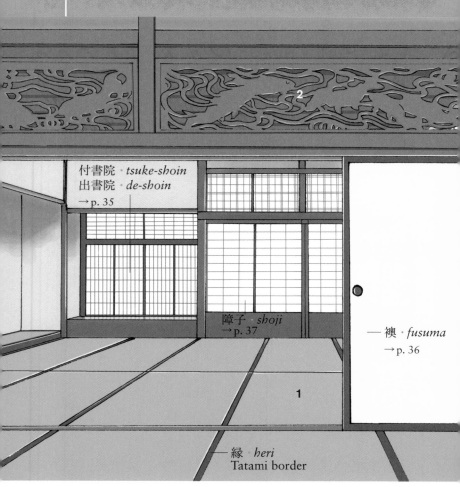

付書院・*tsuke-shoin*
出書院・*de-shoin*
→ p. 35

2

障子・*shoji*
→ p. 37

1

── 襖・*fusuma*
→ p. 36

── 縁・*heri*
Tatami border

Tatami rooms

Until the Muromachi period, wooden floorings were common. As the *shoin-zukuri* style developed, tatami rooms became more popular. The *tokonoma* alcove (page 34), a characteristic of today's Japanese-style room, also developed during this time.

1

畳 ・ *tatami*

Tatami

稲藁（いなわら）などを重ねた畳床（たたみどこ）を、藺草（いぐさ）を織り込んだ畳表（たたみおもて）で覆い、長辺に布の縁（へり）を縫いつけたもの。古くなったら、新しい畳表を張り替える。地方によって畳の大きさが異なり、「京間」「江戸間」などがある（82頁参照）。六畳、八畳のように、座敷の広さは畳の枚数で表わす。

Tatami is basically comprised of three parts: the *tatami-doko*, *tatami-omote* and the *heri*. The *tatami-doko* is the base which is made of multilayered rice straw. This base is covered with the *tatami-omote* which is woven out of rush grass. The *heri*, a cloth border, is woven around the edges. When the mats become old, the *tatami-omote* are replaced with new ones. The sizes of tatami mats differ in each region. (Refer to page 82.) Rooms with tatami mats are called *zashiki*, and their size is measured by the number of tatami mats.

2

欄間 ・ *ramma*

Decorative transom

天井と鴨居（33頁）の間にある開口部分。格子や彫刻を施した板をはめて装飾する。採光・風通しの役割も担う。

A *ramma* is the opening between the ceiling and the lintel (page 33). It is decorated with wooden latticework or carved wood and provides light and ventilation.

鞘の間 · *saya-no-ma*

Sheath room

座敷の外側に設けられた細長い部屋で、畳敷きになっている。本来は、本堂と鞘堂（本体を覆うように建てた建築物）との間にある細長い空間を指す。

A *saya no ma* is a long and narrow room adjacent to the tatami rooms. It has tatami mat floorings.

1

鴨居 · *kamoi*

Lintel

襖（36頁）や障子（37頁）のような建具をはめるために溝をつけられた、上部の横木。

A *kamoi* is a wooden bar with a groove situated above the opening between rooms to fit in opaque sliding doors (page 36) and paper sliding doors (page 37).

2

敷居 · *shiki-i*

Door sill

鴨居に対して、建具をはめるために溝をつけられた下部の横木。

Contrary to *kamoi*, *shiki-i* is situated at the bottom.

3

長押 · *nageshi*

Frieze rail

柱の上部に水平方向に打ち付けた横木のこと。鴨居の上にある。かつては構造補強の意味を持っていたが、現在では装飾の意味が大きい。

A *nageshi* is a wooden beam on the wall which is adjusted to the upper columns, above the lintel. Although it once served as reinforcement of the houses, today it has become more of a decoration.

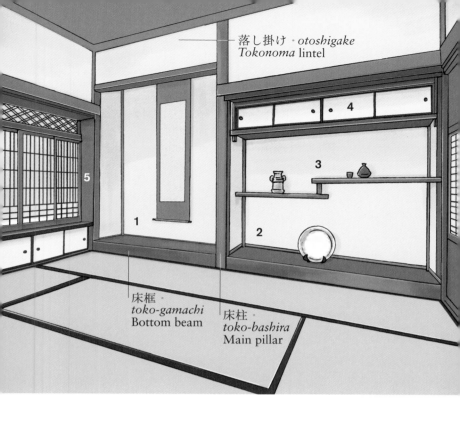

落し掛け・*otoshigake*
Tokonoma lintel

5

4

3

1

2

床框・
toko-gamachi
Bottom beam

床柱・
toko-bashira
Main pillar

1

床の間・*toko-no-ma*／床・*toko*

Alcove

座敷の上座にあって、掛物（99頁）や花などを飾る空間のこと。広い座敷
では、脇床として違い棚や付書院（つけしょいん）が付随する場合もある。

A *toko no ma* is a built-in space located opposite of the entrance in a tatami room. The rear of the room is called *kamiza* and is for the most important guest or person. The alcove is used for displaying a hanging scroll (page 99) and flowers. In a large tatami room, shelves or writing desks are sometimes built next to the alcove.

_____ 2

脇床・*waki-doko*／床脇・*toko-waki*
Side alcove

掛物などを飾るメインの床の隣に設けられる床。違い棚をつけることが
多い。必ずしも付設されるものではない。

A *waki-doko* is a space that is sometimes built beside the main alcove.
Staggered shelves are often attached here.

_____ 3

違い棚・*chigai-dana*
Staggered shelf

ものを飾るために、2枚の棚板を段違いにしてつけたもの。

A *chigai-dana* is a shelf with two boards built in a staggered manner. It is
used for displaying objects.

_____ 4

天袋・*ten-bukuro*／袋戸棚・*fukuro-todana*
Ceiling cabinet

違い棚の上部、天井に接した戸棚のこと。脇床によく見られる。一方、
違い棚の下部にある、地面に接した戸棚のことを「地袋」という。

A *ten-bukuro* is a cabinet above the staggered shelves, adjacent to the
ceiling. It is often built in the side alcove. The cabinet on the floor below
the shelves is called *ji-bukuro*. *Ten* means "heaven" and *ji* means "earth"
in Japanese.

_____ 5

付書院・*tsuke-shoin*／出書院・*de-shoin*
Built-in desk

室町時代の書院造りで、読み書きをするための机となる棚板と明り取り
の障子を出窓風に設けた部分。棚板をつけない場合は「平書院」という。

A *tsuke-shoin* is a space with sliding paper doors to let in the light like a
bay-window and a built-in board which is used as a writing desk. It is seen
in *shoin-zukuri* style during the Muromachi period. When there is no
board, this place is called *hira-shoin*.

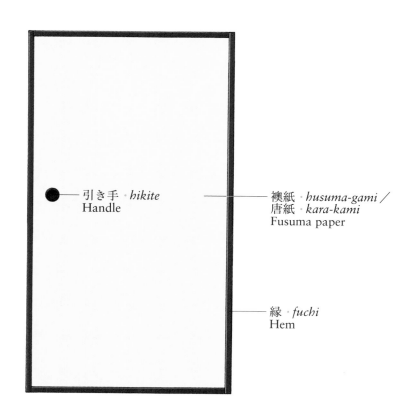

引き手・*hikite*
Handle

襖紙・*husuma-gami*／
唐紙・*kara-kami*
Fusuma paper

縁・*fuchi*
Hem

襖・*fusuma*

Opaque sliding door

格子に組んだ木枠の両面に和紙を下貼りし、厚手の襖紙を上貼りした引き戸。紙のなかでも版木と絵具で模様を摺り出した和紙を「唐紙」といい、襖紙の代名詞にもなっている。

A *fusuma* is a type of sliding door. On both sides of a wooden grid frame, Japanese paper is applied as a foundation. This is then covered with thick *fusuma* paper as the final surface. Japanese paper with patterns printed by using printing blocks and special coloring materials is called *Kara-kami*, which has become synonymous with *fusuma* paper.

Sliding doors

Sliding doors are an important element of Japanese architecture. They can be removed easily to divide space freely.

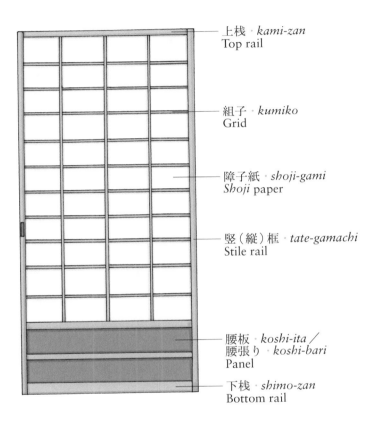

上桟 · *kami-zan*
Top rail

組子 · *kumiko*
Grid

障子紙 · *shoji-gami*
Shoji paper

竪（縦）框 · *tate-gamachi*
Stile rail

腰板 · *koshi-ita* ／
腰張り · *koshi-bari*
Panel

下桟 · *shimo-zan*
Bottom rail

障子 · *shoji*

Paper sliding door

格子に組んだ木枠の片面に、透光性のある薄い和紙を張った引き戸。広義には襖や衝立（95頁）も障子に含まれる。そのため襖は「襖障子」とも呼ばれる。

A *shoji* is a type of sliding door with thin translucent Japanese paper attached to one side of a wooden grid frame. Sliding solid doors and screens (page 95) can also be considered as a type of *shoji*, which is why *fusuma* is also known as *fusuma-shoji*.

日本建築

窓

日本建築にはさまざまな形の窓があり、それぞれに役割を持つ。
その一部を紹介する。

武者窓・*musha-mado*

Warrior's window

武家屋敷の敷地内にある、表通りに面
した建物の外壁に設けられた窓。屋敷
を警護する者が、太い格子の間から外
の様子を窺う。

Musha-mado are barred windows on
the outer walls of a samurai's house,
facing the main street. Individuals
guarding the house checked the outside
scene from between the window grilles.

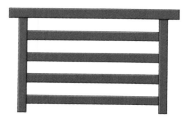

与力窓・*yoriki-mado*

Slatted window

横の格子が入った窓。武者窓と同様に、
武家屋敷の外壁などに設けられた。名
前の由来は、江戸時代の与力（町奉行
を補佐し、司法や警察の任にあたる役
職）の役宅によく用いられたことから
とされる。

Yoriki-mado are slatted windows with
horizontal bars. As is the case with
musha-mado, these were also on the
outer walls of a samurai's house.

下地窓・*shitaji-mado*
塗り残し窓・*nurinokoshi-mado*

Exposed frame window

壁を塗り残して、下地組みを露出させ
た窓。茶室によく取り入れられる。

Shitaji-mado are windows made by
leaving part of the wall's framing
visible. They are often seen in tea rooms.

Windows come in various shapes in Japanese architecture, each with its own unique role. Here are some examples.

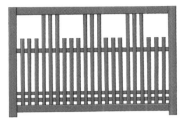

格子窓・*koshi-mado*
出格子・*degoshi*
Lattice window

格子窓の内側からは外がよく見え、外からは中を見えにくくする構造になっている。「竪子（たてこ）」と呼ばれる桟の太さや組み方には、さまざまなバリエーションがある。

These windows are made so that it is easy to look outside but difficult to peek inside.

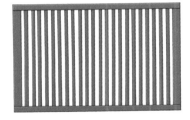

連子窓・*renji-mado*
Barred window

断面が方形もしくは菱形に見える材（連子）を、縦もしくは横に同間隔で連ねた窓。

Renji-mado are windows with vertical or horizontal parallel bars, the cross sections of which are square, or diamond shaped.

火灯（花頭）窓・*kato-mado*
Firelight window

古くは中国から伝わった禅宗寺院の建築に用いられたが、日本の建築物にも取り入れられた。

These windows were seen in Zen-sect temples that came from China. They were then brought into Japanese architecture.

天井

日本建築の天井にはさまざまな組み方がある。ここではその一部を紹介する。

格天井・*gou-tenjo*
Coffered ceiling

格子状に仕切る木材「格縁（ごうぶち）」を組んで、板を張ったもの。
The ceiling boards are held by intersecting chamfered wooden poles.

鏡天井・*kagami-tenjo*
Mirror ceiling

格縁を使わずに、鏡のように板を平面に張ったもの。
The ceiling boards are held without using poles which makes this type of ceiling resemble the flat surface of a mirror.

The ceilings of Japanese architecture have many variations. Here are some examples.

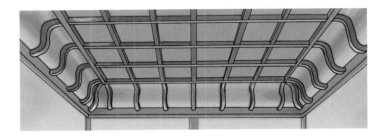

折上天井 · *oriage-tenjo*

Coved ceiling

天井面を、湾曲した材を使って回り縁（天井の縁）から上へ持ちあげたもの。
The ceilings are bent so that the center area becomes higher than the frame.

棹縁天井 · *saobuchi-tenjo*

Board and batten ceiling

回り縁に細い木材や竹などの「棹縁（さおぶち）」を等間隔に渡し、上に天井板をのせたもの。日本の伝統的な建築物で最も一般的な天井。
The ceiling boards are held by thin wooden or bamboo poles that are placed at regular intervals. This is the most common type of ceiling in Japanese traditional architecture.

風呂

火山列島で温泉が湧きやすく、入浴の習慣が根付いている日本人は独自の風呂文化を築いてきた。ここでは家庭以外での代表的な風呂の形式を紹介する。

銭湯・*sento*
Public bath

入浴料を払って入る日常の公衆浴場。「銭（せん）」は江戸時代の最低価値の貨幣の名前。江戸時代以前は蒸し風呂だった。現在は休憩所、食事処などを伴うさまざまな浴場があり、「スーパー銭湯」「健康ランド」とも呼ばれる。

A *sento* is a public bath where people pay entrance fees to take a bath. The word *sen* is the smallest monetary unit used during the Edo period. Today, some public baths have lounges and restaurants. They are called "super *sento*" or "*kenko* (health) land."

ペンキ絵・*penkie*
Mural painting

銭湯の浴場内でよく見られる、壁にペンキで描かれた絵のこと。定番の絵柄は富士山。大正時代に東京のキカイ湯という銭湯に描かれたのが始まりで、それが評判となってほかの銭湯へも広がったとされる。

A *penkie* refers to the painting on the wall of a bathing area in a *sento*. The most classic painting is that of Mt. Fuji. It is said that the first mural painting of its kind was painted on the wall of a *sento* named Kikai-yu in Tokyo during the Taisho period. It attracted attention and spread to other places.

Baths

Japan is a volcanic island country with many hot springs. Bathing in hot water has been an important part of the Japanese people's lives and is also unique to the culture of this country. Here, Japanese baths that can be seen out of ordinary homes are introduced.

風呂

Baths

風呂桶 · *furo-oke*

Bath bucket

浴槽の湯を掬って身体にかけるための桶。底板の回りに、木の板を筒状に並べ、たがで締めた容器を「桶」というが、プラスチック製のものも多い。浴槽自体を風呂桶とも呼ぶ。

A *furo-oke* is a bucket used for scooping water out of the bath tub and pouring it over oneself. *Oke* refers to buckets with wooden boards adjusted around the base plate in a cylindrical manner by using hoops made from material such as bamboo. Today, plastic buckets are also popular. The term *furo-oke* may also be used to refer to the bathtub.

片手桶 · *katate-oke*

Single-handled bath bucket

片側にだけ取っ手のついた桶のこと。片手で湯を掬うことができる。

A *katate-oke* is an *oke* with a single handle so that there is no need to use both hands when scooping hot water.

日本建築

43

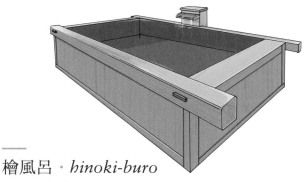

檜風呂 · *hinoki-buro*
Cypress bath

檜材を組んでつくられた浴槽のこと。檜は豊かな香りを持ち、特有の精油成分によって殺菌・防虫能力が高く、浴槽や建材に適している。日本では最高級の建材とされる。

A *hinoki-buro* is a bathtub made from cypress. Cypress is favored for baths or as construction material due to its rich scent. It is also recognized for its essential oil's disinfection effect and repelling of insects. In Japan, cypress is considered to be a top-class building material.

五右衛門風呂 · *goemon-buro*
Cauldron bath

火を焚く竃(かまど／25頁)の上に鉄釜を据えて、円筒形の木桶をのせたもの。もしくは、絵のように釜をそのまま浴槽にしたもので、これを「長州風呂」とも呼ぶ。五右衛門風呂の名前の由来は、安土桃山時代の大盗賊・石川五右衛門が釜茹での刑に処されたことから。鉄底が熱いので、底板を使って入る。

There are two types of *goemon-buro*. One is a cylindrical wooden bucket placed over an iron cauldron, heating it on a cooking stove (page 25) from below. The other uses an iron cauldron as the bathtub, as shown in the picture. This is also called *choshu-buro*. *Goemon-buro* is named after Ishikawa Goemon, a thief in the Azuchi Momoyama period who was boiled to death. Since the bottom of the bathtub is very hot, a wooden board is placed on top of the iron bottom when bathing.

露天風呂・*roten-buro*／野天風呂・*noten-buro*

Open-air bath

屋外にある開放的な風呂のこと。石で組まれた岩風呂がイメージされやすい。自然に湧き出た野湯（のゆ）に浴槽を整備したことから始まったとされる。いまではたいていの温泉施設に露天風呂が備えられている。

A *roten-buro* is a bath placed outside. A popular one is built with rocks. It is said that open-air baths first began when bathtubs were placed outdoors to make use of natural hot springs. Today, open-air baths are a major feature of hot spring facilities.

茶室

茶室とは、客を招いて抹茶でもてなすための建築。基本の広さは
四畳半で、それ以下だと「小間」、それ以上だと「広間」と呼ばれ
る。侘びた雰囲気を持つ独特の建物である。

外観
The exterior of a tea hut

下地窓 · *shitaji-mado*
→ p. 38

連子窓 · *renji-mado*
→ p. 39

Tea huts

The tea hut is an establishment for entertaining guests with powdered green tea. The size of a common tea hut is 4 and 1/2 tatami mats. Smaller ones are called *koma* (small room), and larger ones are called *hiroma* (wide room). This unique architecture has a special atmosphere brought about by its simplicity and quietness.

1

躙口 · *nijiri-guchi*
Crawl-through entrance

およそ縦70cm、横65cmの客用の出入り口。出入りするためには頭を低くする必要があり、謙虚な気持ちを体現することになる。昔は躙口付近に「刀掛け」という棚があり、武士はここに刀を預けてから入室した。ただし、高貴な人専用の「貴人口」を設けている茶室もある。

A *nijiri-guchi* is an entrance for guests. It is approximately 70 centimeters high and 65 centimeters wide. Guests need to lower their heads when coming in and out of this entrance. This makes them embody a feeling of modesty. In the old days, a shelf was attached outside this entrance for samurais to place their swords before entering the hut.

2

土間庇 · *doma-bisashi*
Pent roof for *doma*

土間に柱を立てて、庇（ひさし）を張り出させた部分。
A *doma-bisashi* is the pent roof supported by pillars.

3

扁額 · *hengaku*
Nameplate

横長の額のこと。茶室では「○○庵」「○○軒」といった茶室の名前などを記して掲げておく。
A *hengaku* is a rectangular frame. It is displayed with the tea hut's name inscribed or written on it.

棹縁天井・
saobuchi-tenjo
→ p. 41

内観
The interior of a tea hut

1

点前座 ・ *temae-za*
Host's place

お茶を点（た）てる人が座る場所。点前（てまえ）とは、抹茶を点てて客に飲んでもらうための一連の手順のこと。

A *temae-za* is the area where the host sits. The term *temae* refers to the steps for making powdered green tea and serving it to the guests.

2

炉畳 · *ro-datami*

Sunken hearth tatami mat

「炉」が備えられている畳。炉とは、炭火を入れて釜の水を沸かすところ。畳の下にあるため、使用しない時期は、炉の上に小さな畳を入れておく。

This is a tatami mat with a sunken hearth. A fire is made with charcoal in this hearth to heat water. When it is not used, a small tatami mat is placed on top to cover the hearth.

3

給仕口 · *kyuji-guchi* ／ 火灯口 · *kato-guchi*

Servant's entrance

茶会の料理「懐石」を給仕するときの出入り口。絵のように、上部が炎のようにカーブを描いているものは「火灯口」という。

A *kyuji-guchi* is the entrance used for bringing in special meals for the tea ceremony. When the opening is arched like the flames of fire, it is called *kato-guchi*.

4

腰張 · *koshi-bari*

Waist-high paper skirting

小間の壁の下方に紙を張ったもの。着物の裾が触れて土壁が落ちるのを防ぐ。国宝の茶室「如庵（じょあん）」は昔の暦を張っているため「暦張の茶室」と呼ばれる。

A *koshi-bari* is a papered skirting on the lower part of the walls in small tea rooms. It is put there for preventing the mud-plastered walls from getting damaged when the sleeves of a kimono brush against them.

5

掛込天井 · *kakekomi-tenjo* ／ 化粧屋根裏 · *kesho-yane-ura*

Sloped ceiling

傾斜した屋根裏を天井の姿に整えた形式。狭い茶室空間を広く見せる効果がある。

A *kakekomi-tenjo* is the sloped ceiling under the attic. This ceiling makes the tea room look spacious.

露地

客を茶室の入り口へと導く庭を「露地」という。木々と石で構成され、日本庭園（56頁）とはまた異なる閑静な趣を持つ。

石灯籠・
ishi-dōrō
→p. 52

柄杓・
hishaku
→p. 71

___
1

蹲踞・*tsukubai*

Washbasin set

清浄な空間である茶室に入る前に、手と口を浄める場所。水をためた手水鉢（水鉢）を中心にして、そのほかに3つの大きな石で構成される。

A *tsukubai* is for purifying the mouth and hands before entering a tea hut. It consists of a stone used as a washbasin with water and three other large stones.

A *roji* is a garden of trees and stones which leads to the entrance of a tea hut. It has a quiet atmosphere different from the tranquility of Japanese gardens (page 56).

— 2
飛石・*tobi-ishi*
Stepping stones

客を茶室へ導くための道しるべとなる石。客が歩きやすいように、計算された間隔で配置されている。

Tobi-ishi are stepping stones that lead guests to the tea hut. They are placed at intervals which make it easy for the guests to walk.

— 3
枝折戸・*shiorido*
Wicket gate

竹や木の框（かまち）に、竹を菱形に組み込んだ戸。木の枝を折ってつくったような簡素な戸を意味する名前。露地の中ほどに設置されることが多い。

A *shiorido* is a gate made by weaving bamboo on bamboo or wooden frames to form diamond shapes. The term literally means simple doors that look as if they are made from broken branches. A *shiorido* is often set in the middle of a tea hut garden.

—
関守石・*sekimori-ishi*／
留め石・*tome-ishi*
Barrier stone

飛石の岐路に置いて、通行止めを意味する石。縄で十文字に結んである。

A *sekimori-ishi* is a stone tied with ropes in crisscross pattern that is placed on a stepping stone. It cautions guests not to go beyond that point.

石灯籠

本来、石灯籠は神社や寺院の境内で使われていた照明。のちに、露地（50頁）や一般の庭園にも据えられるようになった。さまざまな意匠があり、ここではその一部を紹介する。

春日灯籠・*kasuga-doro*

奈良県・春日大社に献納された石灯籠と同形のものを「春日灯籠」と総称する。六角柱の火袋（火を灯すところ）に笠と宝珠がのり、竿と呼ばれる脚がつく。火袋の2面に雌雄の鹿、他の2面に日月が彫られている。

A *kasuga-doro* is a lantern that comes in the same form as the stone lanterns in Kasugataisha Shrine in Nara prefecture.

雪見灯籠・*yukimi-doro*

丈が低く、笠が大きい庭園用の石灯籠。池のほとりなどによく置かれている。脚の数は、四本、三本、二本とバリエーションがある。

A *yukimi-doro* is a small stone lantern with a large roof. They are placed in gardens often near the edge of ponds. The number of legs can be two, three or four.

Stone lanterns

Stone lanterns were originally used as lighting in the grounds of shrines and temples. Later, they came to be placed in tea hut gardens (page 50) and gardens of ordinary houses. Here are some examples of the various lantern designs.

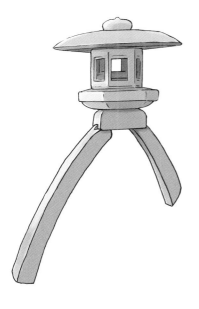

琴柱（徽軫）灯籠・ *kotoji-doro*

雪見灯籠が変化した2本脚の灯籠。琴の糸を支える「柱（じ）」に似ていることから名が付いた。金沢・兼六園にある「徽軫（ことじ）灯籠」が有名で、本来、2本脚は同じ長さだったが、片足が折れたためいまの形になったとされる。

A *kotoji-doro* is a two-legged lantern that developed from *yukimi-doro*. The name of this lantern comes from its shape which resembles a *kotoji*, the pillars of *koto* (a Japanese harp). A famous *kotoji-doro* is the one in Kenroku-en in Kanazawa prefecture.

塔灯篭・*to-doro*

塔のような形をした灯籠。三重塔、五重塔のようなものもあれば、幾重にも笠が連なっている形態もある。

A *to-doro* is a lantern shaped like a pagoda. Some are three-storied or five storied and others may have more roofs.

日本の垣根は竹や木を組んだものと、植栽を利用した生垣に大別される。敷地の境界を示したり、なかの建物を隠したりする役割があるが、その多様な意匠も注目される。

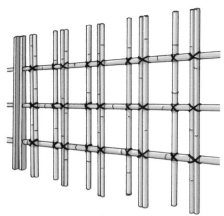

四つ目垣・*yotsume-gaki*

丸太の支柱の間に、竹を縦横に組んで四つ目（四角形）に隙間をあけたもの。

A *yotsume-gaki* is a type of fence with bamboo fixed vertically and horizontally on log columns so it forms square lattices.

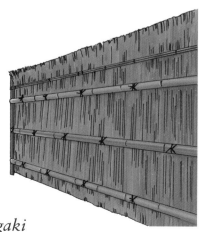

萩垣・*hagi-gaki*

萩を縦にまとめて、横向きにした竹で固定したもの。

A *hagi-gaki* is a fence made by gathering bush clover vertically and fixing them together with horizontal bamboo poles.

Fences

Japanese fences can be categorized into two types: those made by weaving bamboo or wood and those formed by hedges. They serve as boundaries or as a means of hiding establishments and come in various designs.

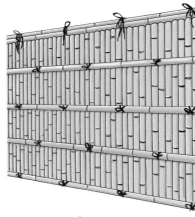

建仁寺垣 · *kenninji-gaki*

竹を隙間なく並べて、横向きにした竹で固定したもの。京都・建仁寺で用いられた形式とされる。

A *kenninji-gaki* is a fence made by placing bamboo together tightly and fixing them with horizontal bamboo poles. This type of fence was first used in Kenninji Temple in Kyoto.

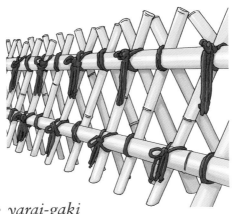

矢来垣 · *yarai-gaki*

竹を斜めに組み合わせて、交差した部分を縄で結んで固定したもの。

A *yarai-gaki* is a bamboo fence with diagonal lattice openings. The crossing points are tied together with rope.

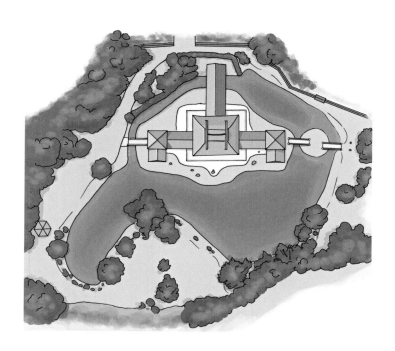

浄土式庭園・*jodoshiki-teien*

Pure land garden

極楽浄土の世界を表現した庭園で、平安から鎌倉時代までに多くつくられた。本堂の前方に大きな池と洲浜状の岸辺があり、池の中島には橋がかけられている。橋はあの世とこの世を繋ぐ役割がある。当時は阿弥陀仏を信仰することで極楽浄土に往生できるという仏教の「浄土思想」が広まっていた。代表的な浄土式庭園として、京都・平等院がある。

A *jodoshiki-teien* is a garden that expresses the Pure Land. Many gardens were built in this style from the Heian to Kamakura periods. In front of the main hall, there is a large pond and a sandy shore. A small island in the middle of the pond is connected to shore by bridges which connects the land of the living and the land of the deceased. It was believed that by having faith in Amida Buddha, one would be able to go to the Pure Land after death. A well-known garden built in this style is the Byodoin Temple in Kyoto.

Japanese gardens

In the past, gardens of temples, shrines and houses of aristocrats were made by drawing water and setting stones. The ideas behind the construction of gardens and its forms have changed over time. Today, various types of gardens exist in historical temples and shrines.

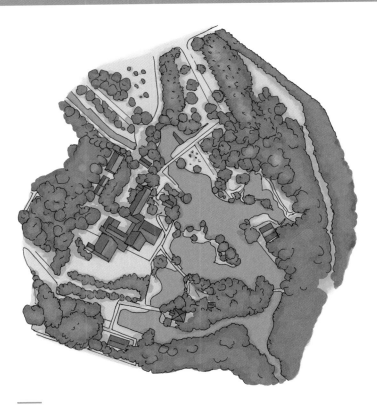

池泉回遊式庭園 · *chisen-kaiyushiki-teien*

Pond-stroll garden

池を中心に園路がめぐらされた庭園。園内には中島や橋、茶室（46頁）などが築かれる。書院造のための庭園で、室町時代から江戸時代にかけて発展した。書院造とは床の間（34頁）のある書院座敷で構成される、武家住宅の様式の1つ。代表的な池泉回遊式庭園として、京都の二条城や桂離宮がある。

A *chisen-kaiyushiki-teien* is a garden with a promenade around a pond which is in the center of the garden. Islands, bridges and tea huts (page 46) are built in the garden. This garden style is for *shoin*-style houses, and it developed from the Muromachi to Edo periods. *Shoin*-style is a style of samurai houses which have tatami rooms with alcoves (pages 34). The Nijo Castle and Katsura Imperial Villa in Kyoto both have representative pond-stroll gardens.

庭の石組
Composition of rocks in a garden

三尊石 · *sanzonseki*
Triad stones

日本庭園では庭石を自然や神仏に見立て、その組み方によって人それぞれの理想の世界を表現する。三尊石は仏像の「三尊形式」のように、中央に背の高い石を据え、両脇にそれよりも低い石を配した石組だが、必ずしも仏の姿を表わしているわけではない。抽象的でなにを表しているのか判別が難しいものもあり、答えがあるとは限らない。

In Japanese gardens, stones are displayed in various ways to represent various ideal worlds. *Sanzonseki* are set so that the tallest stone stands in the center with smaller stones at both sides resembling Buddhist statues or images. However, they do not necessarily represent the Buddha. Often it is difficult to identify what these stones represent, and there isn't always an answer.

沢渡石・*sawatari-ishi*

Stepping stone

池のなかに置かれた石。踏み石としての実用性と景観を併せ持つ。日本庭園における池は、海や川を表現している。

Sawatari-ishi are stones placed in ponds. While they serve as stepping stones, they also create the scenery. Ponds in Japanese gardens express the ocean and rivers of the real world.

砂盛 • *sunamori*
Raked gravel mound

砂を円錐形に盛ったもの。枯山水庭園では島や山を表わす。

A *sunamori* is sand formed into a conical shape. In dry landscape gardens, they express islands and mountains.

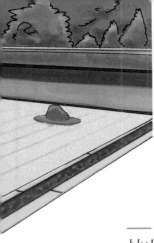

枯山水庭園 · *karesansui-teien*
Dry landscape garden

水を使用せずに、主に白川砂と石組などで山や海、川、滝を表現した庭。室町時代以降、禅宗寺院の隆盛とともに成熟していった。「石庭（せきてい）」とも呼ばれ、その代表的なものとして、京都・龍安寺（りょうあんじ）の石庭がある。

A *karesansui-teien* is a garden without water, which uses gravel and rocks to express moutains, the ocean, rivers and waterfalls. It is also called *sekitei* (rock garden). A representative garden of this type is the Ryoanji Temple in Kyoto.

砂紋 · *samon*
Raked gravel patterns / sand patterns

水の動きを白砂で表わした紋様。砂用の熊手や箒を使って、さまざまな紋様を描く（「箒目をつける」ともいう）。その一部を62～63頁で紹介する。

Samon are patterns made by sand that express rippling water and waves. Rakes and brooms are used to create various patterns, some of which are introduced on page 62 and 63.

砂紋の種類
Types of *samon* patterns

青海波紋 · *seigaiha-mon*

Blue ocean wave

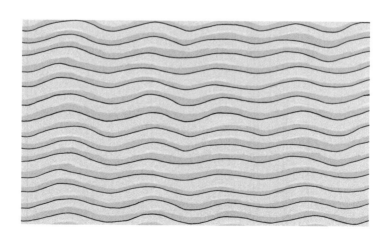

流水紋 · *ryusui-mon*

Flowing water

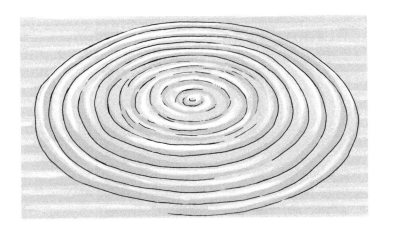

水紋 · *sui-mon*

Water ripple

——

荒波紋 · *aranami-mon*

Raging wave

城

城（城郭）は戦国時代から江戸時代にかけて、武家が外敵の侵入を防ぐために築いた砦のこと。さまざまな形式があり、現在見られる城の多くは石垣や堀、天守を持った江戸時代のものである。

1

天守・*tenshu*

Castle tower

城に築かれる瓦葺きの高層建築。砦としての大型の櫓（やぐら）を織田信長が「天守」という3、4階建ての豪華な建築物に革新した。屋根は入母屋造り（20頁）を主に、複雑に構成されるが、大屋根が3つある天守は「三重の天守」という。天守にはさまざまな形態がある。

A *tenshu* is the highest castle tower with tiled roofs used as a watchtower. Nobunaga Oda, a feudal warlord, reinvented *tenshu* into an imposing architectural structure of three to four stories high.

Castles

Castles were built by samurai families from the Warring States period to the Edo period as fortresses against enemies. Although their styles vary depending on each period, most of the castles that are left today are ones from the Edo period with stone hedges, moats and towers.

2

櫓 • *yagura*

Turret

城郭における櫓とは、矢などの武器を納めたり（矢蔵）、物見（監視）をするための建造物のことを指す。天守と同様に瓦屋根を使った櫓は、屋根の数によって「平櫓」「二重櫓」「三重櫓」と呼ばれ、三重櫓は天守の代用にもなる。役割によって「渡櫓」「物見櫓」「付櫓」などの名前がある。

A *yagura* built in the castle grounds was an establishment which served as a storehouse for weapons and as a watchtower. Tile-roofed *yagura* had different names depending on the number of roofs: *hira-yagura* (one story-high), *niju-yagura* (two stories-high) or *sanju-yagura* (three stories-high). A *yagura* with three roofs can serve as a *tenshu*.

城

Castles

鯱 • *shachihoko (shachi)*

Shachihoko ornaments

天守の最上部の屋根にある、想像上の生き物「鯱（しゃちほこ／しゃち）」を模した火除けの飾り。現代でも見ることのできるマイルカ科のシャチとは別の生き物で、虎の頭を持ち、胴体は魚である。雨を降らすことができるという言い伝えから掲げられたとされる。

A *shachihoko* is an ornament that adorns the topmost roof of a *tenshu*. This *shachihoko* (*shachi*) is an imaginary animal which has the head of a tiger and the body of fish. It was told that this imaginary creature could make rain fall, which is why these ornaments were put up as charms to save the castle from fire.

日本建築

鳥居
Shinto gateway

神明鳥居・*shimmei-torii*
Shimmei-style gateway

鳥居とは2本の柱を貫（ぬき）で連結し、その上に笠木（横材）を渡したもの。直線的でシンプルな神明鳥居は、伊勢神宮系の神社でよく見られる形。鳥居は神域と俗界を隔てる境界として、神社の入り口に立てられる。

A *torii* is built by connecting two columns with a horizontal rail. Another horizontal rail is passed over this. This linear and simple Shinmei-torii can often be seen in shrines that are related to the Ise Shrine. *Torii* are constructed at the entrances of shrines as borders to divide the sacred and the secular worlds.

Shrines

Shrines are for enshrining the gods in Shinto, an indigenous religion of Japan. Each shrine consists of a main establishment where the gods are enshrined as well as several other constructions. Nature, animals and human beings are all worshipped in shrines since it is believed that gods are everywhere in Shintoism.

明神鳥居 · *myojin-torii*
Myojin-style gateway

最も一般的な鳥居。貫が2本の柱を貫通し、笠木（横材）が端に向かってゆるやかに曲線を描いている。

A *myojin-torii* is the most common type of *torii*. A horizontal rail penetrates the two columns, and the second rail is passed over in a slight upward curve towards the edges.

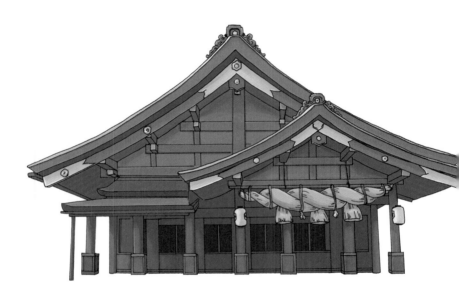

大社造り・*taisha-zukuri*
Taisha-style

切妻造り（20頁）の屋根で、妻側（19頁）が正面になる「妻入り」の社殿。妻側の右または左に入り口がある。島根県・出雲大社に代表される、神社建築において最古の形式の1つである。

Taisha-zukuri is a style of constructing the main building of a Shinto shrine. It has a gabled roof (page 20) and the gable end wall (page 19) is at the front of the structure. The entrance is located on either side of the gable end wall. It is one of the oldest styles of shrine construction that can be represented by the Izumo Taisha Grand Shrine in Shimane prefecture.

神明造り · *shimmei-zukuri*

Shimmei-style

切妻造りの屋根で、平側（19頁）が正面になる「平入り」の社殿。棟木の
上に装飾材「堅魚木（かつおぎ）」が多く並んでいるのが特徴。三重県・
伊勢神宮に代表される形式である。

Shimmei-zukuri is a style of constructing the main building of a Shinto
shrine. The exterior wall (page 19) that is parallel to the main ridge is at the
front of the structure. Shrines built in this style have ornamentation called
katsuogi on roof ridges. The Ise Shrine in Mie prefecture is a representative
shrine of this style.

流造り・*nagare-zukuri*
Nagare-style

神明造り（69頁）のように切妻造り（20頁）の屋根で「平入り」の社殿だが、屋根の前流れが後ろに比べて長いのが特徴。全国の神社で最も多く見られる構造で、京都の上賀茂神社、下鴨神社などに代表される形式である。

Nagare-zukuri has a gabled roof (page 20) and an entrance on the exterior wall that is parallel to the main ridge, as with *Shimmei*-style (page 69). It is unique in that the front slope of the roof is longer than the back. *Nagare*-style is the most common style in shrines throughout Japan, such as Kamigamo-jinja and Shimogamo-jinja shrines in Kyoto.

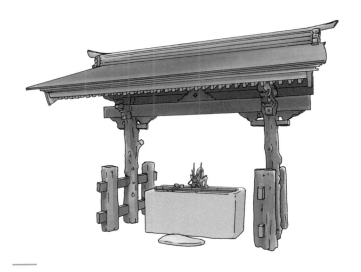

水盤舎・*suibansha* ／ 手水舎・*chozuya*

Hand-washing shelter

参拝者が本殿でお参りする前に手や口を浄めるための施設。一般的な手水の仕方は①左手を洗う、②右手を洗う、③左手に水を受けて口をすすぐ、④再度左手を洗う、⑤水を入れた柄杓を立てて柄を洗う、という順番で行う。

A *suibansha* is a small pavilion for cleansing the hands and mouth before entering the main sanctuary. Common steps are: 1. hold the ladle with your right hand, scoop water and pour it over your left hand; 2. hold the ladle with your left hand to rinse your right hand; 3. take water in your left hand to rinse your mouth; 4. rinse your left hand again; 5. rinse the handle with water by tipping the ladle.

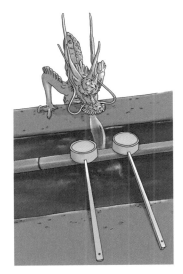

柄杓・*hishaku*

Ladle

水や液体を汲む道具。水を入れる部分を「合（ごう）」という。竹製が一般的だが、木製や金属の簡易的なものもある。神社の柄杓は合を伏せて置くが、露地の蹲踞（つくばい／50頁）の柄杓は合を横向きに置く。

A *hishaku* is used for scooping water or other liquid. The cupped part for holding water is called *gou*. They are generally made of bamboo, but some are made of wood or metal.

賽銭箱 · *saisen-bako*
Offertory box

社殿の前に置かれたお賽銭（金銭）を入れるための箱。本来は金銭ではなく、自然の恵みに感謝して海や山の幸、特に米を紙で包んで神様に供えていた。いまでも、お賽銭で感謝の気持ちを表わしてから、次の願い事をするのが正しい参り方である。

A *saisen-bako* is a box placed in front of the shrine's main building for throwing in offering coins. Before these offertory boxes were used, rice wrapped in paper or blessings from the ocean or the sea were offered to show gratitude to nature. When tossing coins, it is important to express feelings of gratitude before making a new wish.

狛犬 · *komainu* ／獅子 · *shishi*
Guardian dogs

神社の門前や社殿の前に置かれた、犬もしくは獅子に似た一対の像。聖域を守る存在である。ペルシアやインド地方が起源とされるため、「異国の犬」という意味で「高麗（こま）犬＝狛犬」と称された。仁王像（77頁）と同様に口を開けているほうが「阿形（あぎょう）」、口を閉じているほうが「吽形（うんぎょう／んぎょう）」と呼ばれる。

Komainu or *shishi* are pairs of dog or lion-like statues that are placed outside the gates or the main buildings of shrines. They are guardians of the sacred area. As is the case with the two Deva Kings (page 77), the one with its mouth opened is called *a-gyo*, and the one with its mouth closed is called *un-gyo*.

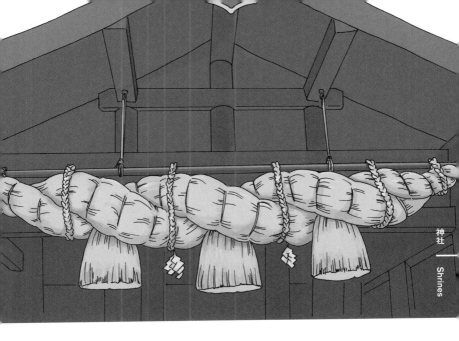

注連縄 · *shime-nawa*

Ritual Shinto rope

神聖な場所との境界を示す藁（わら）の縄。神社以外にも、正月に自宅の玄関に飾ったりする。島根県・出雲大社の巨大な注連縄が有名。

A *shime-nawa* is a straw rope that forms a boundary between the sacred and the secular worlds. In addition to use in shrines, these ropes also decorate entrances of ordinary houses for the New Year. The ritual Shinto rope at Izumo Taisha Grand Shrine in Shimane prefecture is well known.

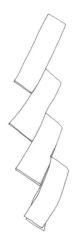

紙垂（四手）· *shide*

Paper streamer

注連縄や神前に供える榊（さかき／129頁）、御幣（ごへい）などにつけて垂らす白い紙。折り方や断ち方にはさまざまな形式がある。邪悪なものを追い払うという。

Shide are white paper streamers attached to ritual Shinto ropes, *sakaki* (cleyera japonica / page129) trees or ritual wands called *gohei* that are offered to god. They come in various shapes. It is said that they keep away evil spirits.

鈴 ・ *suzu*

Bell

参拝の際、鈴緒を振って鈴を鳴らすことで、神様を招く。また、鈴の清々しい音色が参拝者を祓い清めるとされる。鈴緒は紅白あるいは5色が一般的。

Worshippers ring the bells at shrines by pulling the ropes hanging from them to call out to god. It is said that the clear sound drives evil spirits away and purifies the worshippers. The ropes are usually red and white or five-colored.

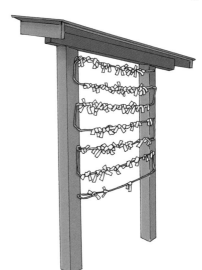

おみくじ・*omikuji*
Fortune slip

神様のお告げを問い、吉凶を占う「くじ」。おみくじの箱を振って、穴からくじを出し、そこに書かれた番号の紙をもらって吉凶を確認する。引いたおみくじは持ち帰るのもよし、定められた所に結んでもよい。昔は境内の木に結んで帰ったそうだが、いまでは木を傷つけないために結ぶ場所が確保されたといわれる。

Omikuji are written fortunes. Worshippers shake boxes which have numbered sticks inside and take out one stick. Then they receive a fortune slip which has the same number as the stick. They can take these slips with them or tie them on a specified place. They were originally tied to trees inside the precincts, but today there are designated places for tying the slips so that the trees are not damaged.

門
Gate

四脚門・*shikyaku-mon*
Four-legged gate

2本の門柱（本柱）の前後に、合わせて4本の控柱（ひかえばしら）がある
門。寺院の建築様式のなかでよく見られる門の形である。控柱が計8本
の「八脚門」もある。

A *shikyaku-mon* is a gate with four bracing struts besides the two main
columns. This is the most popular type of gate seen in temples. There are
also eight-legged gates with eight bracing struts.

Temples are constructed in various ways, influenced by history and different sects. This section will be an introduction to gates, Buddhist Sanctums and pagodas specific to temples.

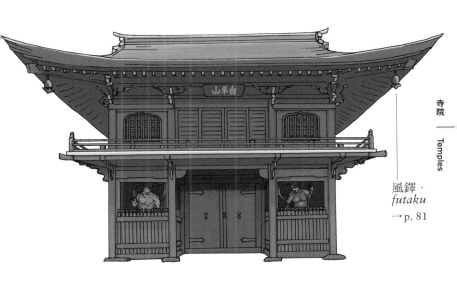

風鐸・
futaku
→ p. 81

楼門・*ro-mon*

Tower gate

屋根が一重で、楼閣風の2階建ての門。高欄（こうらん）付きの回り縁（周囲を取り巻く縁）が、上層と下層の間についている。屋根が二重になっていると「二重門」と呼ばれる。

Ro-mon are two-storied gates with one roof. Deck railings are attached to the ceiling molding that goes around the structure between the first and second stories. *Ro-mon* with two roofs are called *niju-mon* (two-storied gate).

仁王像・*niozo*

Two Deva Kings

仏教における守護神の一対の像。「金剛力士像」という名前だが、二体一対のときには「仁王（二王）」とも呼ばれる。狛犬（72頁）と同様に、向かって左に「阿形（あぎょう）」、右に「吽形（うんぎょう／んぎょう）」がある。

A *nio-zo* is a pair of guardian statues in Buddhism. This type of statue is called *kongo-rikishi zo*. When these statues come in a pair, they are called *nio* which means "two kings." Like the guardian dogs (page 72), the statue on the right is *a-gyo* and the statue on the left is *un-gyo*.

仏殿・*butsuden*

Buddhist sanctum

仏像を安置し、礼拝するための本堂。

A *butsuden* is the main hall for placing the statue or image of Buddha.

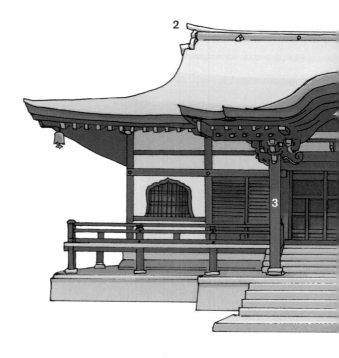

1

懸魚・*gegyo*

Fish-shaped gable ornament

破風に取り付けられた飾り板。
いろいろな形があるが、本来は、
火災に遭わないようにという願
いを込めて水と関わりのある魚
の形にしたため、この名が付い
たとされる。

Gegyo are decorative wooden
boards attached to the roof
gable. Although they come in
various shapes, they were
originally shaped like fish as a
charm to prevent fire.

2

鳥衾・*toribusuma*

Ornamental roof tile

大棟や降棟（18頁）の先端に突
き出した瓦のこと。鬼瓦（19
頁）の上についている。

Toribusuma is a type of roof tile
that sticks out of the end of
ridges. They are attached on top
of the ridge-end tiles (page 19).

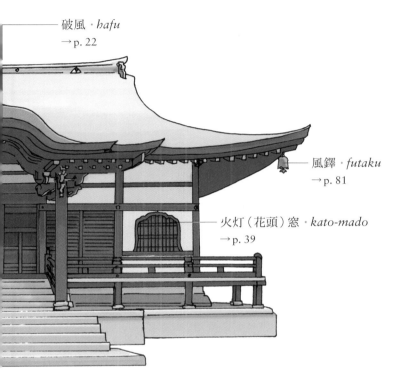

破風・*hafu*
→ p. 22

風鐸・*futaku*
→ p. 81

火灯（花頭）窓・*kato-mado*
→ p. 39

3

向拝柱・*kohai-bashira*

Kohai column

流造り（70頁）の屋根のように、前に張り出させた屋根と、その下の空間を「向拝」といって拝礼空間となる。その屋根を支える柱を「向拝柱」という。

Roofs that stick out such as *Nagare*-style (page 70) roofs are called *kohai* together with the space under these roofs where worshippers pray. The columns that support such roofs are called *kohai-bashira*.

五重塔・*goju-no-to*
Five-storied pagoda

仏塔は舎利（仏陀や聖人の遺骨）、経典などを納める高層建築。三重塔、五重塔をはじめ、十三重まで奇数の屋根の塔がある。釈迦の遺骨を安置するために建立されたインドのストゥーパに由来するとされる。日本最古は奈良県・法隆寺の五重塔である。

Pagodas are high towers for keeping sutras and the remains of Buddha or saints. Pagodas always have an odd number of stories. Starting from three-stories, they can be up to thirteen-stories high. It is said that the origin of Japanese pagodas are the stupas in India where the remains of Buddha are kept. The oldest five-storied pagoda in Japan is that of Horyuji Temple in Nara prefecture.

___
1

相輪・*sorin*
Metal pagoda decorations

仏塔の上部にある金属の装飾部分。下から、露盤（ろばん）、伏鉢（ふせばち）、請花（うけばな）、九輪（くりん）、水煙（すいえん）、龍車（りゅうしゃ／竜舎）、宝珠（ほうじゅ）の7パーツからなる。

Sorin is a term for referring to the metal decorations on the top part of a pagoda.

___
2

風鐸・*futaku* ／
宝鐸・*hotaku (hochaku)*
Wind bell

仏殿や仏塔の軒の四隅に吊らされる、青銅製で鐘形の鈴。風鈴（ふうりん）と似たもの。

Futaku are bronze bells hung under the eaves of Buddhist Sanctums and pagodas. They resemble *furin* wind bells.

畳のサイズ
The size of tatami mats

日本人は部屋の広さを「○○畳」と言って、畳の枚数で把握してきた。現在では畳のある住宅は少なくなってきたが、それでも床の上で生活する日本人のライフスタイルは畳に影響を受けているとされる。ここでは、地域によって異なる畳のサイズについて紹介する。

In Japan, room sizes have been measured with the number of tatami mats. Although there are not many houses with tatami rooms today, the Japanese lifestyle is influenced by tatami mats. Here, we will introduce various measurements of tatami mats that differ according to region.

京都を中心とした関西圏
京間（本間・関西間）＝6尺3寸（約191cm）×3尺1寸5分（約95.5cm）

Kansai region (mainly Kyoto)
Kyo-ma tatami (hon-ma, kansai-ma): approximately 191 centimeters by 95.5 centimeters

名古屋を中心とした中部地方
中京間＝6尺（約182cm）×3尺（約91cm）

Chubu region (mainly Nagoya)
Chukyo-ma: approximately 182 centimeters by 91 centimeters

関東圏を中心とした東日本
江戸間（関東間）＝5尺8寸（約176cm）×2尺9寸（約88cm）

East Japan (mainly Kanto region)
Edo-ma (kanto-ma): approximately 176 centimeters by 88 centimeters

その他の畳
団地畳＝マンションや団地に合うように、小型化した畳のこと。5尺6寸（約170cm）×2尺8寸（約85cm）ほどの大きさ。
琉球畳＝現在では半畳サイズの畳を指すことが多い。本来はシチトウという植物を畳表に使用した畳のことをいい、シチトウの畳表を使用していれば1畳サイズの畳も琉球畳と呼ぶ。

Other tatami mats
Danchi-datami: A tatami mat made smaller to fit apartments. It is approximately 170 centimeters by 85 centimeters.
Ryukyu-datami: Today, tatami mats that are half the normal size are called *ryukyu-datami*. Before, tatami mats with *tatami-omote* made from Shichito matgrass were called *ryukyu-datami*, regardless of whether they were full size or half size.

生活道具

JAPANESE TRADITIONAL EVERYDAY THINGS

桐簞笥・*kiri-tansu*

Paulownia-wood chest of drawers

簞笥とは衣類や道具を収納するための引き出しがついた家具。衣装簞笥には、畳んだ着物を入れる特別な引き出しがついている場合もある。軽量で防虫性が高く、内部の湿度も一定に保つ桐材は、衣装簞笥の定番になっている。花嫁の両親が嫁ぎ先に簞笥を贈る風習があり、「嫁入り簞笥」とも呼ばれる。

A *tansu* is a chest of drawers for clothing and utensils. Some wardrobes have special drawers for keeping folded kimonos. Paulownia wood is light, repels insects and keeps the interior humidity stable which makes it a popular wood for chests of drawers.

Furniture

Japanese traditional furniture is made to accommodate traditional Japanese clothing while sitting on tatami mat floors. Although not commonly used in modern homes today which have been westernized, they are used in Japanese style inns, restaurants and homes.

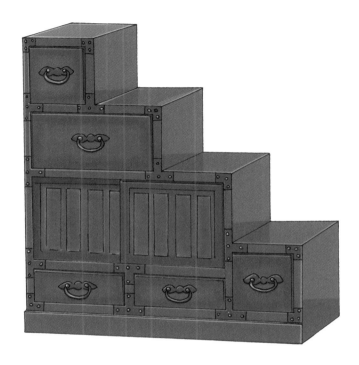

階段箪笥・*kaidan-tansu*／箱箪笥・*hako-tansu*
Staircase chest

家屋の階段の側面に引き出しをつけた箪笥。現在ではインテリアとしての家具になっている場合もある。道具箪笥には用途に応じてさまざまな形があり、雑多なものを入れる用箪笥や手元箪笥、茶の道具などを入れる茶の間箪笥（茶箪笥）、漢方薬を入れる薬箪笥などがある。なかには、火事などに備えて、紐付きや車輪付きの可動式もあった。

A *kaidan-tansu* is a chest of drawers made by attaching drawers on the side of the stairs inside a house. Today, there are chests of drawers built to resemble stairs as an interior. Chests come in various forms depending on the use such as those for keeping random everyday things, tea utensils or medicine. Some have ropes or wheels attached to make them easier to move or carry in case of fires.

飾り棚・*kazari-dana*

Ornamental shelf

文房具や美術品などを飾るための棚。なかでも、三段式で二枚の開き扉がある物入れ（厨子／ずし）を中段と下段につけた「厨子棚」「三棚」と呼ばれるものは、武家や公家の道具として普及した。

A *kazari-dana* is a shelf for displaying stationery and art. Those that are three-tiered with double-door cabinets called *zushi* on the middle and bottom levels are called *zushi-dana* or *san-dana* (three shelves). They were common in houses of samurais and court nobles.

衣桁・*iko*

Clothing rack

着物や帯など衣服をかけておく道具。イラストは床に直接立て、二つ折りにできるものだが、さまざまなスタイルがある。着物用ハンガーは「衣紋（えもん）掛け」ともいう。

An *iko* is a clothing rack for kimonos and obis. Among various types, the picture shows one which can be set on the floor and bent in the middle so that it fits in the corner of a room. Hangers for kimonos are called *emon-kake*.

鏡台・*kyo-dai*
Dressing table

化粧や髪結いのときに用いる。
化粧品や髪結いの道具などを入
れておく小箪笥の上に鏡がつい
ている。

A *kyo-dai* is used for applying
makeup or for doing one's hair.
A mirror is attached on top of a
small chest of drawers in which
cosmetics and hair ornaments
can be stored.

家具 | Furniture

姿見・*sugatami*
Full-length mirror

全身を写す細長い鏡。イラスト
のように観音開きの扉がついて
いる姿見もある。鏡は江戸時代
中期までは銅などの金属板を磨
いたものであったが、後期から
は現代にも通じるガラス鏡を使
い始めたとされる。

A *sugatami* is a full-length mirror which sometimes has double
doors as shown in the picture.
Up until the middle of the Edo
period, mirrors were made of
polished metal such as copper. It
is said that it was during the latter
part of the Edo period and on-
wards that glass, as we see today,
began to be used for mirrors.

生活道具

卓袱台・*chabu-dai*

Low dining table

畳に座って食事をするときのテーブル。円形が多く、脚を折り畳んで片付けることができる。江戸時代は脚付き膳や箱膳を一人ずつ使っていたが、近代になって、家族で卓袱台を囲むのが日常の風景になった。

A *chabu-dai* is a low dining table used in tatami rooms. People sit directly on tatami mats when using this table. Many come in round shapes and the legs can be folded in for putting the table away. In the Edo period, small wooden boxes which served both as a table for one and as storage for keeping tableware were used for meals. In modern Japan, it became common for families to eat together at a *chabu-dai*.

座卓・*zataku*

Low table

座敷用の脚の短いテーブル。主に接客用の部屋で用いる家具だったため、天板の周囲や脚に装飾的な文様が彫られていることが多い。

A *zataku* is a low table for tatami rooms. Since this type of low table is mainly used in drawing rooms, decorative designs are often curved around the tabletop and in the legs.

座布団・*zabuton*
Floor cushion

畳に敷く、木綿綿（もめんわた）が
入ったクッション。木綿の生産量
が増えた江戸時代に普及した。そ
れ以前は藺草（いぐさ）や藁（わ
ら）でつくった敷き物（円座）を使
っていた。

A *zabuton* is a cotton cushion for
tatami rooms. These cushions became popular in the Edo period
when cotton production increased
in Japan. Before this time, round
cushions made from rush or straw
were used.

座椅子・*zaisu*
Legless chair

脚のない背もたれ。上に座布団を
敷いて、座卓用の椅子とする。現
在でも旅館や料亭でよく見られる。

A *zaisu* is a chair with a normal
chair back but with no legs. It is
used with a floor cushion. This
type of chair is used for low tables
and is often seen in Japanese style
inns and restaurants.

脇息・*kyosoku*
Armrest

座敷に座ったときに、身体の脇に
置いて肘をもたせ掛ける肘掛け。イ
ラストのように、肘を置く部分に
は綿入りの織物が張ってある場合
もある。

A *kyosoku* is an armrest that is
placed on tatami mats. As the picture shows, some have a cotton pil-
low attached.

南部鉄瓶・*nambu-tetsubin*
Nambu iron kettle

火箸・*hibashi*
Tongs

銅壺・*doko*
Copper boiler

関東火鉢・*kanto-hibachi*
長火鉢・*naga-hibachi*
Rectangular brazier

炭を燃料とする暖房具「火鉢」のうち、長方形の箱型のもの。脇が机になっており、その下に引き出しがついている。イラストのように、灰の上に「銅壺（どうこ）」と呼ばれる湯沸かし器を備えているものもある。

A *hibachi* is a charcoal brazier. Rectangular ones have a small table on the side with drawers below. As the picture shows, some have copper boilers called *doko* placed above the ashes.

火箸・*hibashi*
Tongs

手焙り・*te-aburi*
Hand-warmer

その名の通り、手を焙るための小形の火鉢。中に灰を入れ、炭火を熾して使う。陶製、木製、石製などさまざまである。灰の上に五徳（3本または4本の脚がある輪）を置いて、鉄瓶をかけて湯を沸かしたり、網をのせて食べ物を焼いたりすることもある。

A *te-aburi* is a small brazier for warming hands. Ashes are put inside to light fire. They can be ceramic, wooden or stone. A trivet can be placed above the ashes on which iron pots are placed for boiling water or grill nets for food.

蚊帳・*kaya*

Mosquito net

蚊や害虫を防ぐための覆い。麻や綿でできている。主に就寝時に使われ、四隅を天井から吊って寝床を覆う。全体が緑色で、赤い縁取りのタイプが一般的。

A *kaya* is a net made from hemp or cotton which is used for keeping away mosquitoes and other insects. These nets are hung from the ceiling on four corners so that they cover the space where people sleep. The most common type is green with a red hem.

蚊取り線香・*katori-senko*
蚊遣り線香・*kayari-senko*
Mosquito coil

蚊を除くための線香。除虫菊（殺虫成分を含む菊）の花や茎などの粉末を糊で固めたもので、長時間燃えつづけるように渦巻状にしたものが一般的。昔は木を燻して虫を追い払うだけの「蚊遣り火」だった。

A *katori-senko* is an incense for repelling mosquitoes. It is made from the flowers and stems of pyrethrum that are pulverized and hardened with glue. These coils often come in spiral shapes to keep them burning for a long time.

蚊取り豚・*katori-buta*／蚊遣り豚・*kayari-buta*
Pig-shaped incense holder

蚊取り線香を入れておく豚型の陶器製容器。内部に針金がついており、そこに蚊取り線香をかけて火をつける。なぜ豚の形になったのかについては諸説ある。

A *katori-buta* is a pig-shaped ceramic incense holder. A wire is attached inside to hook a mosquito coil. There are various views on why it is pig-shaped.

葛籠・*tsuzura*

Lacquered wicker box

ツヅラフジの蔓や竹などを編んでつくられる箱状の物入れ。上から紙を
張り、漆を塗ったものが定番。衣服などを入れる。

A *tsuzura* is a wicker box made by weaving the vines of Sinomenium acu-
tum or bamboo. The most common type is covered with paper and lacquered. It is used for storing clothing.

行李・*kori*

Wicker box

竹や柳を編んでつくられる箱状の物入れ。葛籠（つづら）の一種。衣類
や旅行用の荷物を入れたりする。ご飯を入れるための小さな行李を「飯
行李」と呼ぶ。

A *kori* is a type of *tsuzura* made by weaving bamboo or willow. It is used
for storing clothes or for travels. A small *kori* used for putting cooked rice
is called *meshi-gori*.

長持・*nagamochi*
Trunk

長方形で木製の大きな物入れ。衣服や調度品などを保存しておく。棹通しがついているため、持ち運びも可能。車輪の付いた巨大なものもあったという。

A *nagamochi* is a large wooden box for storing clothing and daily necessities. It can be carried around by sliding in a pole through the rings attached to the box. Some are large with wheels.

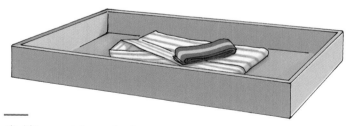

乱箱・*midare-bako*
乱衣装箱・*midare-isho-bako*
Clothing box

脱いだ衣服やこれから着る衣服を入れるための浅い箱。寝室や更衣室に置く。木製が一般的。平安時代の公家の調度品である「打乱箱（うちみだりばこ）」が原型とされ、衣服や手拭いを入れたり、髪を梳くときに使っていた。現在では旅館でよく見られ、部屋着（浴衣）などが入れてある。

A *midare-bako* is a shallow box used in bedrooms and changing rooms for storing clothing to wear or clothing that have been taken off. These boxes are generally made of wood. Today they are often seen in Japanese style inns, where they are used for storing *yukata*.

衝立・*tsuitate*

Screen

室内を仕切ったり、目隠ししたりするために立てるもの。シンプルな木製のものや、竹製、葦（あし）製、桟の入ったもの、襖（36頁）や障子（37頁）のようなものなどさまざまな意匠があり、衝立自体が部屋の装飾を兼ねている。玄関や座敷の境目、寝室の入り口などに置かれることが多い。

A *tsuitate* is a screen used for dividing space or hiding areas inside the house. These screens can be made from wood, bamboo or reed, and come in various designs such as those with frames or those that look like opaque (page 36) or paper (page 37) sliding doors. They are part of the decoration inside a house and are often placed at entrances of houses and bedrooms or as partitions between tatami rooms.

曲・*kyoku* ／ 扇・*sen*

前奥手・*mae-ode*

屏風・*byobu*
Folding screen

襖（36頁）のように格子に紙を貼ったものを、2つ以上連結させた衝立（95頁）の一種。2枚折りのものを「二曲屏風」といい、就寝時に枕元に立てたりする。イラストのような「六曲屏風」は座敷に飾る美術品としても用いられる。六曲屏風2枚で一対となるものを「六曲一双屏風」と呼ぶ。

A *byobu* is a type of screen which consists of more than two *fusuma* (page 36)-like screens connected. Folding screens that can be folded in two are called *nikyoku-byobu* and are placed at the head of one's sleeping mat. The picture shows a type called *rokkyoku-byobu*, a six-fold screen which is often used as art for decorating tatami rooms.

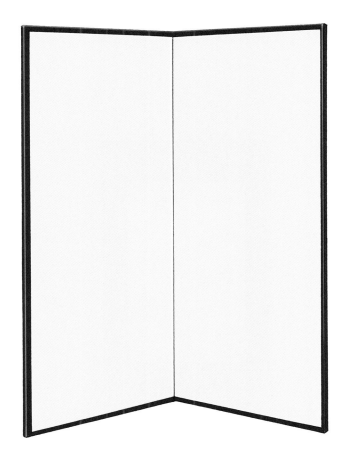

勝手屏風・*katte-byobu*
水屋屏風・*mizuya-byobu*
Screen for kitchen

縦長の二曲屏風。台所（勝手／水屋）の前に立てて、客人から台所が見えないようにするために用いる。

A *katte-byobu* is an oblong two-fold screen. It is placed in front of the kitchen to prevent the guests from seeing into the kitchen.

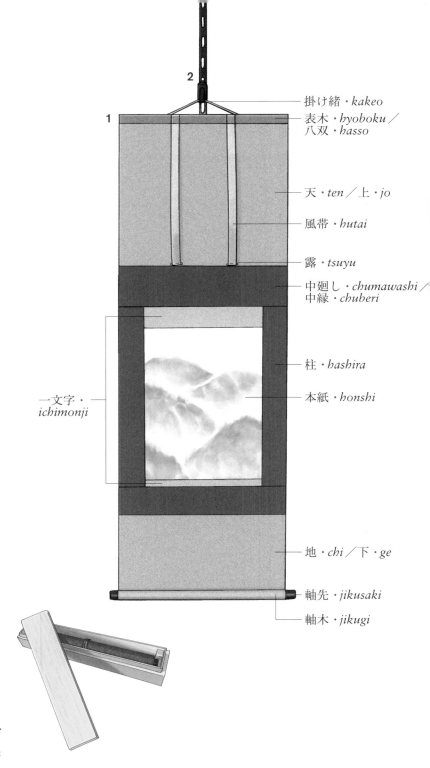

掛け緒・*kakeo*

表木・*hyoboku*／
八双・*hasso*

2

1

天・*ten*／上・*jo*

風帯・*hutai*

露・*tsuyu*

中廻し・*chumawashi*／
中縁・*chuberi*

柱・*hashira*

一文字・
ichimonji

本紙・*honshi*

地・*chi*／下・*ge*

軸先・*jikusaki*

軸木・*jikugi*

——1

掛物・*kakemono*
掛け軸・*kakejiku*
Hanging scroll

床の間に掛けて飾る書画のこと。書画を裂（きれ／布）で縁取りして軸を取り付け、巻き納めることができるようになっている。季節や客人に合った掛物を掛けてもてなす。使用しない場合は、丸めて専用の箱に入れて保管する。

A *kakemono* is a painting or calligraphic work that is hung in the alcove. It has fabric edges and a scroll attached so that it can be rolled up and stored. Different hanging scrolls decorate the alcove for different seasons and guests. When not used, they are stored in special boxes.

——2

自在・*jizai*
Adjusting hook

床の間に軸を掛けるときに、高さを調整するための道具。金属製、竹製、木製の細長い自在に可動式の釘がついていて、ちょうどよい高さに釘を調節して軸の紐（掛け緒）を掛ける仕組み。

A *jizai* is a tool for adjusting the height of hanging scrolls. A sliding hook is attached to a metal, bamboo or wooden pole, on which the strings attached to a scroll can be hung. This hook can be moved to adjust the height.

灯火具

昔の灯火具の火種は植物油やロウソクで、屋外で使用するものは風除けのために和紙（108頁）や絹を張った囲いの中に入れた。これを「行灯（あんどん）」と呼び、用途に応じて種類がある。

足元行灯・*ashimoto-andon*

Foot lamp

行灯のうち、足元に置いて足場を照らすためのもの。現在では旅館の庭や通路、露地（50頁）などで使われる。

An *ashimoto-andon* is placed at one's feet. Today, it is used in the gardens or passages of Japanese-style inns, or in tea hut gardens (page 50).

Lamps

Traditional lamps burned vegetable oil or candles for illumination. Therefore, lampshades made from *washi* paper (page 108) or silk were used to avoid wind when these lamps were used outside. Such lamps are called *andon*, and there are various types depending on the purpose.

短檠 · *tankei*
Short oil lamp

油と灯芯でともす灯り。灯芯とは綿糸でできた紐状のもの。「雀瓦（すずめがわら）」と呼ぶ器に油を入れ、灯芯を浸して火をつける。現在では夜の茶席で目にすることがある。

A *tankei* is a type of oil lamp which uses a string wick made of cotton. Oil is poured in a container called *suzume-gawara*, and the wick is dipped in this oil to fuel the flame. Today, it can be seen in tea ceremonies.

手燭 · *teshoku*
Portable candlestick

持ち手（柄）をつけたロウソク立て。現在でも、夜に行う茶会で用いられる。

A *teshoku* is a candlestick with a handle. Today it is used in tea ceremonies that are held at night.

生活道具

提灯・*chochin*

Paper lantern

なかにロウソクを入れて提げて使う行灯（あんどん）。持ち手の先にぶら提げて夜道を照らす「馬乗り提灯」、祭礼で使う「祭り提灯」、折り畳むと箱状になる「小田原提灯」、盆行事で仏壇を飾ったり、先祖の霊を迎えるときに使用する「盆提灯」など、さまざまな形状や用途がある。

Paper lanterns are a type of *andon* which have candles inside and are hung from places or held by the hand. They come in various shapes and have different purposes. An *umanori-chochin* is used for lighting the way when riding horses, a *matsuri-chochin* is used for festivals, an *odawara-chochin* can be folded up and a *bon-chochin* is used for decorating the Buddhist family altar during the Bon festival or for welcoming the spirits of ancestors.

盆提灯・*bon-chochin*

祭り提灯・*matsuri-chochin*

馬乗提灯・*umanori-chochin*

小田原提灯・*odawara-chochin*

文房具

現在、「書道用品」とされる道具も、かつては日常使いのもの。墨、硯、筆、紙は「文房四宝（ぶんぼうしほう）」と呼ばれる。

筆 · *fude* ／ 毛筆 · *mohitsu*

Writing brush

羊、鹿、馬、狸などの毛を、それぞれの弾力・長さ・強度を考えながら組み合わせて穂をつくり、持ち手となる軸（筆管）をつける。筆の種類は多種多様。

The head of a *fude* is made from the hair of animals, such as sheep, deer, horses and racoon dogs. Softness, length and durability are considered when these hairs are mixed. The holder called a *hikkan* is attached to this. Writing brushes come in numerous types.

Stationery

Tools that are specifically for Japanese calligraphy today were daily items in the past. Ink, inkstones, writing brushes and paper for Japanese calligraphy were considered to be the four indispensable items.

—— 2

筆架・*hikka*

Brush rest

筆の先を架けて休ませておく台のこと。

A *hikka* is a brush rest to place the brush by its tip.

—— 3

墨・*sumi*

Ink

煤（すす）に膠（にかわ／ゼラチン）と香料を加えて固めたもの。もしくはそれを水にすって液体化したもの。菜種や胡麻などの油を燃やして採った煤を使う「油煙墨」、松脂（まつやに）を燃やして採った煤を使う「松煙墨（しょうえんぼく）」がある。

Sumi is ink made by mixing gelatin, soot and perfume. It is made solid but must be dissolved in water to be used.

—— 4

硯・*suzuri*

Inkstone

石を彫ってつくった、墨をするための道具。「墨磨（すみす）り」という意から名が付いた。硯の上に水をたらし、固形の墨をこすることにより、煤が溶け出して墨汁ができる。

A *suzuri* is a special stone for rubbing ink. By rubbing solid *sumi* on this stone with a few drops of water, the soot contained in the solid ink dissolves into water and becomes liquid ink.

—— 5

硯屏・*kembyo*

Screen for inkstone

硯のそばに立てて、塵や埃が入るのを防ぐ小さな衝立屏風。

A *kenbyo* is a small screen set near the inkstone to prevent dust from getting in the ink.

文房具

Stationery

生活道具

水滴 · *suiteki*
Dropper

硯に入れる水をためておく器。
A *suiteki* is a container for keeping water to use on an inkstone.

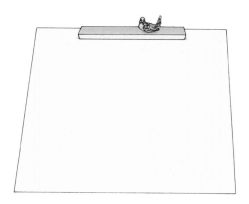

文鎮 · *bunchin*
Paperweight

和紙が動いたり、風で飛んだりしないようにのせるおもし。
A *bunchin* is the Japanese term for paperweight.

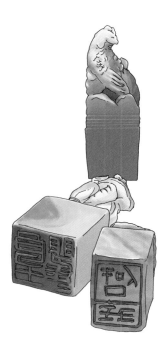

印章・*insho*
印鑑・*inkan*
Stamp

文字やシンボルなどを彫り、朱をつけて印影を転写し、個人や職責の証とするもの。象牙、石、木などの素材でつくられる。イラストのような落款（らっかん／117頁）用の印章を彫ることを「篆刻（てんこく）」という。

An *insho* is a stamp made by engraving letters and symbols on ivory, stone, wood, etc. This is stamped with vermilion ink as a sign for the author of a work. Engraving a stamp for *rakkan* (page 117), as shown in the picture, is called *tenkoku*.

印泥・*indei*／印肉・*in-niku*
Inkpad

印章につける朱肉のこと。銀朱に油分を溶かし、ヨモギや紙を加えて練り固めてつくられる。現在、一般に使用されているのは、スポンジに朱の液を染み込ませたもの。朱印を入れてある容器全体を印池（いんち）、または肉池（にくち）という。

Indei is vermilion ink for stamps. Traditionally, vermilion pigment was mixed with mugwort and Japanese paper to make this ink. Today, red sponge inkpads are more common.

和紙 · *washi*

Washi paper

楮（こうぞ）など樹皮の繊維を原料にしてつくられる、日本古来の手漉き紙。強靭で変質しにくいため保存に向いているとされる。文字や絵を書くだけでなく、包みに用いたり、文化財の補修にも使用されたりする。福井県の越前和紙や岐阜県の美濃和紙が有名。

Washi is made from the fiber of the bark of trees, such as paper mulberry. It is a traditional Japanese handmade paper. Since this paper is strong and retains its original state, it is said to be suited for preservation. It is not only used for writing or drawing, but also for wrapping things up or for repairing cultural assets. Echizen *washi* in Fukui prefecture and Mino *washi* in Gifu prefecture are both representative *washi* paper.

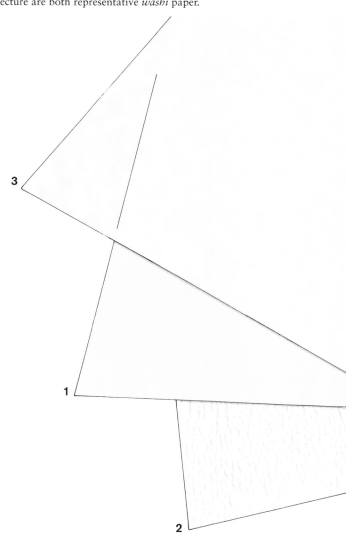

1

奉書紙 ‧ *hoshoshi*
Ceremonial *washi* paper

楮を原料とした真っ白で厚手の上質紙。室町幕府が公文書として用いたことから「奉書」と呼ばれた。現在市販されている祝儀袋（122頁）などの儀礼用の包みによく使われている。

Hoshoshi is a white and thick high-grade *washi* paper made from the fiber of mulberry. This paper was used by the Muromachi shogunate for official documents. Today, it is often used as material for envelopes used in ceremonious occasions, such as *shugi-bukuro* (page 122).

2

檀紙 ‧ *danshi*
High-grade *washi* paper

厚手で表面に縮緬（ちりめん）状のしわがある最も格の高い和紙。結納や高額の祝儀袋に使用されることが多い。

Danshi is a thick crepe paper and it is the highest-ranking *washi* paper. It is often used for *shugi-bukuro* when wrapping betrothal money or large amounts of money.

3

半紙 ‧ *hanshi*
Half-sized *washi* paper

習字用の紙。本来は杉原紙（現在の兵庫県杉原谷でつくられていた和紙）を半分に裁断したためにこの名が付いたが、現在は縦約35cm、横約25cmの書道用和紙の総称となっている。

Hanshi is a paper used for Japanese calligraphy. The word *hanshi* uses characters that mean "half" and "paper." This is because *hanshi* was originally made by cutting in half a type of *washi* paper produced in today's Sugiharadani, Hyogo prefecture. Today, *hanshi* is used as a general term to refer to paper for Japanese calligraphy that is approximately 35 centimeters long and 25 centimeters wide.

千代紙 · *chiyogami*
Chiyogami

和紙（108頁）にさまざまな色柄を木版で刷った華やかなもの。京千代紙と江戸千代紙がある。京千代紙は有職（ゆうそく）模様などの伝統的な柄で、江戸千代紙は格子柄や紋尽くしなど大胆な柄のものが多い。

Chiyogami is *washi* paper (page 108) with colorful woodblock print motifs. There are two types: *chiyogami* that was produced in Kyoto and *chiyogami* that was produced in Edo, which is the old name for Tokyo. The former had traditional patterns, such as those used for clothing and furniture owned by nobles. The latter had more bold designs such as lattice patterns or patterns using various family crests.

折り紙・*origami*
Origami

紙を折って動植物などを象る技法、遊び。和紙で贈りものを包む伝統的な作法「折形（おりがた）」から発展したもので、本来は祈りを捧げるためにつくる。病気の治癒や延命を祈りながら、鶴を千羽折る「千羽鶴」は有名。

Origami is an art of folding paper to make things such as animals and plants. It developed from *origata*, a traditional method of wrapping gifts with *washi* paper. Origami was originally for making wishes. *Sembazuru* is a well-known tradition, in which one thousand paper cranes are made to wish for long life and recovery from illness.

短冊 · *tanzaku*
Paper strip

俳句や短歌などを書くための細長い紙のこと。市販品のサイズは縦約36cm、横約6cm。

Tanzaku is a strip of paper for writing traditional Japanese poems. The most common size is around 36 centimeters long and 6 centimeters wide.

色紙 · *shikishi*
Paperboard

和歌や寄せ書きに使われる、ほぼ正方形の厚紙。よく目にする市販品の「大色紙」は縦約27cm、横約24cm。

A *shikishi* is a square cardboard used for writing traditional Japanese poems or messages from a number of people. The most common size is around 27 centimeters long and 24 centimeters wide.

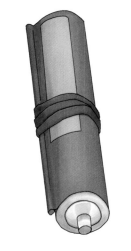

巻子 · *kansu*
Washi scroll

和紙を横に貼りつないで布などで補強し、端に軸をつけたもの。軸を芯にして巻物状にする。昔の絵巻物の多くが巻子である。構造は掛物（99頁）に似ている。

A *kansu* is a hand scroll made by sheets of *washi* paper joined in sequence and supported with cloth on the backside. Most traditional picture scrolls were made in this form.

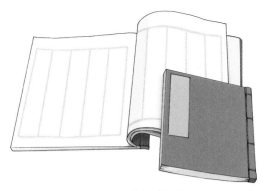

和綴じ本・*watoji-bon*／和装本・*waso-bon* 和帳・*wacho*

Japanese-style book

2枚に折った紙を重ね、その束の天地に角布を貼ってから表紙とともに糸で綴じた本もしくは帳面。日本で古くから行われてきた製本方法である。和綴じにはさまざまな種類があり、糸の掛け方には最も一般的な「四つ目綴じ」のほか、「亀甲綴じ」「高貴綴じ」などがある。

A *watoji-bon* is a book made by layering paper folded in half, attaching cloth to the corners and binding them together with the cover by using strings. This is a traditional bookbinding that has been practiced in Japan for a long time. It has various styles.

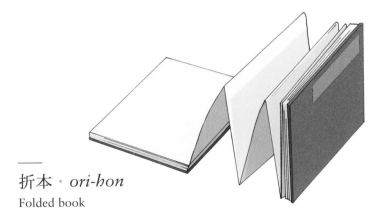

折本・*ori-hon*

Folded book

横に貼りつないだ紙面を端から畳折りにした、綴じ目のない本。代表的なものは経典の折本で、両面にお経が書かれている。白無地の折本は御朱印帳にも用いられている。御朱印とは、寺社に参拝した際にその証として授け与えられる印のこと。

An *ori-hon* is an accordion fold book without bindings. A representative book of this type is the book with Buddhist scriptures, which has scriptures written on both sides of the paper. *Ori-hon* with plain white pages are used for collecting red seals which are given at shrines and temples.

美術品の箱

日本には、大切な道具や美術工芸品を木の箱に入れてしまってお
く伝統的な習慣がある。ルーツは仏具を納めるための箱とされる。
桐製が一般的。

Boxes for art

Storing precious utensils and art objects in wooden boxes is a custom that has been around for a long time. It is said that this originally comes from how Buddhist altar fittings were stored in wooden boxes. Such boxes are commonly made of paulownia wood.

1

箱書 · *hako-gaki* ／書付 · *kakitsuke*
Box inscription

箱の蓋の表もしくは裏側に書かれた文字のこと。収納する作品の名前や作者名、所蔵者などを墨（105頁）と筆（104頁）で書き記す。箱書はその作品の伝来を示し、権威付けを行うことに繋がる。

Hako-gaki are letters written with a writing brush (page 104) in *sumi* ink (page 105) on the outer or inner side of the lid of a box. It tells the name of the art object inside the box, the author and the owner. A *hako-gaki* is proof of where the art comes from and gives authority to it.

2

真田紐 · *sanada-himo*
Sanada himo cord

太い木綿糸を平組みにした紐のこと。茶道具や美術工芸品の箱に真田紐が付属している場合が多い。安土桃山時代の武将・真田昌幸が発明したことから名が付いたとされる。非常に丈夫なため、本来は刀の柄巻きや下げ緒に使われていた。

A *sanada-himo* is a flat cord woven from heavy cotton thread. It is often attached to boxes for storing tea utensils and art objects. The name is said to have come from Masayuki Sanada, a warrior in the Azuchi-Momoyama period, who invented this cord. Since it is very sturdy, it was originally used for wrapping the handles of Japanese *katana* swords or as safety cords attached to scabbards.

3

四方掛け結び · *yoho-kake-musubi*
Four-direction knot

方形の箱に取り付けられた紐を結ぶ際の、最も一般的な結び方。正面から見ると蝶結びになる。

This is the most common style of tying a cord on a square box. It is tied so that there is a bow.

美術品の箱　Boxes for art

生活道具

115

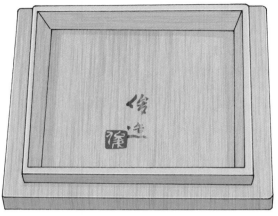

1

2

1

桟蓋 · *sambuta*
Framed lid

裏側に桟のついた蓋で、桟の部分を箱の口の内部にはめ込んで蓋をする。
四方桟と二方桟がある。

A *sambuta* is a lid framed on the interior. When it is put on a box, the frame
fits inside the box so that the lid closes tightly. It comes in two types: framed
on parallel sides or on all four sides.

2

落款 · *rakkan*／落成款識 · *rakuseikanshi*
Signature

作者が美術品の完成後に記入した書名、印、花押（かおう／サイン）など
の総称。正式名称は「落成款識（らくせいかんし）」。

A *rakkan* is a signature, a seal or a mark called *kao* that is placed on an art
object by its creator.

香道具

仏教とともに、中国から伝来したとされる香文化。現代では「香りを聞く（嗅ぐ）」ことを作法として愉しむ「香道」にまで発展した。ここでは、香道で用いる道具の一部を紹介する。

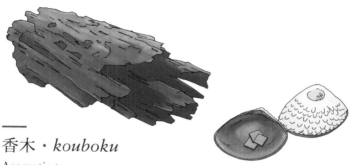

香木・*kouboku*

Aromatic tree

熱に触れると芳香を放つ木のこと。沈香（じんこう）や白檀（びゃくだん）などが知られるが、いずれも東南アジアで産する特殊かつ希少な樹木で、日本では採集できない。小さく割った小片に熱を加えて、香りを聞く。

A *kouboku* is a tree that generates fragrance when heated. Agarwood and sandalwood are representative aromatic trees. However, they cannot be collected in Japan since they are rare and unique to Southeast Asia. The trees are broken into small pieces, which are heated to generate fragrance.

練香・*nerikou*

Solid perfume

粉末状の香料に、蜜や梅肉、甘葛（あまづら）などを加えて練り固めたもの。香料は香木のほかに丁子（クローブ）、麝香（じゃこう／ムスク）、貝香などがある。練香は香りを部屋に漂わせる際に使う。

A *nerikou* is made by mixing powdered incense with nectar, pureed Japanese plum pickles, etc. In addition to aromatic trees, cloves, musk and sea shells are also used as incense. Solid perfume is used as room fragrance.

Utensils for incense ceremonies

The culture of incense was introduced to Japan from China, together with Buddhism. Today, it has developed into an art of enjoying fragrances.

香炉・*kouro*
聞香炉・*kiki-kouro*
Incense burner

香をたくための器。陶器製、金属製などさまざまである。なかに灰を入れ、火をつけた炭団（たどん／120頁）を埋めて、その上に銀葉と香木を置いて香りを漂わせる。香炉を左手のひらにのせ、右手で口縁を覆い、その隙間から香りを聞く。

A *kouro* is an incense burner made from various material such as ceramic or metal. Ashes are laid inside, and a piece of lit charcoal (page 120) is buried in the ashes. A thin sheet of silver and a piece of aromatic tree is placed on top. The fragrance is enjoyed by holding the burner with the left hand and covering the opening slightly with the right so that the fragrance comes out from beneath.

銀葉・*gin-yo*
Silver sheet

薄い雲母（うんも）の板に、銀、錫（すず）など金属の縁をつけたもの。その上に香木の小片をのせる。香道の手前では、銀葉挟（ぎんようはさみ）という専用のピンセットで銀葉を扱う。

A *gin-yo* is a thin sheet of mica with metal edges such as silver and tin. A piece of aromatic tree is placed on this *gin-yo*. When practicing the art of incense, *gin-yo* is handled with special tweezers.

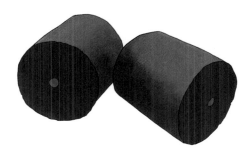

炭団・*tadon*／香炭団・*kou-tadon*

Charcoal

木炭の粉末をふのりなどで固めて乾燥させた燃料。香道以外で使われる炭団（たどん）は球状である場合が多い。香道で使用する香炭団は木炭のような形をしている。

A *tadon* is fuel made by solidifying charcoal powder with glue plant. It is shaped like a charcoal when practicing the art of incense. For other occasions, it comes in a sphere.

折据・*orisue*

Card wrapper

香道の手前や茶道の点前で使用する札を入れておく包み。紙を折り畳んでつくられており、上部を開くと箱状になる。香道では「組香（くみこう）」といって、数人が集まって数種の香木をたき、香りを聞き分けて愉しむ会で、正解だと思う札を入れていくときに使用する。

When several people gather for practicing the art of incense, there is a game in which they try to tell one incense from another. Special cards are used for this game. The cards have personal symbols on one side for indicating to whom the cards belong and numbers on the other side which are used for giving answers. An *orisue* is used for keeping these cards.

銀葉盤・*gin-yo-ban*

Tray for *gin-yo*

銀葉（119頁）をのせるための漆塗りの台。香をたくごとに銀葉を変えるので、たく香の数だけ、あらかじめ銀葉を準備しておく。イラストのような花の形をしたものは貝あるいは象牙でできており、その上に銀葉をのせる。

A *gin-yo-ban* is a small lacquered tray for placing *gin-yo* (page 119). The parts shaped like flowers as shown in the picture are made of shells or ivory, on which *gin-yo* are placed.

源氏香之図・*genjiko-no-zu*／源氏香・*genjiko*

The Genjiko chart

5種類の香木を用いて、5つの香炉で焚いた香りを聞き分ける組香「源氏香」の答えを表す図形のこと。5本の縦線が5つの香炉を表し、同じ香りと思った香炉同士を横線で繋ぐと52通りの図になるので、『源氏物語』54帖のうち最初と最後を除いた巻名を、その図形に当てはめている。図形は文様としておもしろく、美術工芸品にも取り入れられている。

A *genjiko no zu* is a chart with special characters that shows the answers to an incense guessing game. This game uses five types of aromatic trees and five different incense burners. The word *genji* comes from a fictional novel written by Murasaki Shikibu in the Heian period, titled "The Tale of Genji." It depicts the rise and fall of court nobles through love stories of the imperial prince, Hikaru Genji. There are 52 different patterns in this chart, each of which are named after the chapters in "The Tale of Genji." Since this novel has 54 chapters, the names of the first and last chapters are not used.

冠婚葬祭で金銭あるいは進物を贈る際に、紙に包んで水引（みずひき／124頁）をかけることが日本のならわし。古くは自ら紙を折っていたが、現在では市販の包みを使用することがほとんど。

祝儀袋・*shugi-bukuro*

Special envelope for celebratory monetary gifts

結婚、昇進、転居などの祝儀（慶事）があった相手に、金銭を贈るための包み。裏側の下部の折り返しを、上部の折り返しの上に重ねるのが決まり。表書きには「御祝」などと書く。

A *shugi-bukuro* is an envelope used for offering money in celebration of events such as marriage, promotion or moving. The lower flap must come over the upper flap on the backside of the envelope.

不祝儀袋・*bu-shugi-bukuro*

Special envelope for monetary gifts as condolences

不祝儀（弔事）があった相手に、金銭を贈るための包み。裏側の上部の折り返しを、下部の折り返しの上に重ねるのが決まり。葬儀の際には表書きに「御霊前」「御佛前」「御香奠（典）」「玉串料」などと書く。薄墨で書く場合もある。

A *bu-shugi-bukuro* is an envelope used for offering money for condolences such as at funerals. The upper flap must come over the lower flap on the backside of the envelope.

Gifts

When offering money or gifts for celebrations, it is traditional in Japan to wrap cords called *mizuhiki* (page 124) around envelopes. Although it is common to buy envelopes with *mizuhiki* cords in stores today, in the past, people used to fold paper to make their own envelopes.

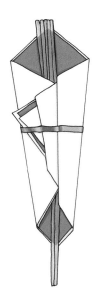

熨斗・*noshi*／折り熨斗・*ori-noshi*
熨斗鮑・*noshi-awabi*
Dried abalone

熨斗鮑とは鮑の身を削り、薄く叩き伸ばして乾燥させたもの。神事の供え物であり、祝儀に欠かせない品物である。その熨斗鮑を紅白の紙で包んだものを「折り熨斗」という。現在よく見られる「折り熨斗」は熨斗鮑が黄色い紙片に替わっているが、本来は本物の熨斗鮑が使われていた。

Noshi-awabi is dried and flattened abalone. It is an offering to god and is indispensable for celebrations. When this dried abalone is wrapped in red and white paper, it is called *ori-noshi*. Today, pieces of yellow paper are used in place of dried abalone for *ori-noshi*.

熨斗紙・*noshi-gami*／掛け紙・*kake-gami*
Noshi wrapping paper for gifts

贈答の品にかける、折り熨斗と水引が印刷された紙。用途に合った水引の色や結び方のものを使う。水引の上に「御祝」など贈答の目的、下に贈り主の名前を書くのが正式。手土産などの軽い贈答品にかける場合には、どちらも書かない「無地熨斗」「素(す)熨斗」でもよいとされる。

Noshi-gami is paper with images of *noshi-awabi* and *mizuhiki* printed on it. It is used for decorating gift boxes. The images of *mizuhiki* come in different colors and shapes, which are chosen depending on the occasion.

水引・*mizuhiki*
Mizuhiki cord

和紙（108頁）のこよりに水糊をひいて乾かし固めたもの。それを束にして包みに結ぶ。祝儀袋には紅白や金銀の水引、不祝儀袋には黒白や黄白、双銀の水引を用いる。用途に応じて結びの形にも決まりがある。

真結び・*ma-musubi*
結び切り・*musubi-kiri*
Square knot

解けることのない、最も格の高い結び。結婚式や葬儀など1度きりであってほしい事柄に使われる。

This is the most formal way of tying *mizuhiki*. It is used for occasions such as weddings or funerals which hopefully happen only once in a lifetime.

両輪結び・
morowana-musubi
Flower knot

蝶結びに似た形で、両端を引っ張るとさっと解ける。何度あってもよい、出産祝いや入学祝などの慶事に用いる。

This is a knot tied like a bow so that it can be loosened easily by pulling both ends. It is used for occasions that people wish to celebrate many times such as births or entrance ceremonies.

A *mizuhiki* is a cord made from *washi* paper (page 108) twisted into strings and starched. Red and white or gold and silver *mizuhiki* are used for envelopes in celebratory events. Black and white, yellow and white, or silver-only *mizuhiki* are used for envelopes in events of misfortune. The cords are knotted in different ways depending on the occasions.

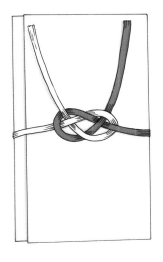

鮑結び・*awabi-musubi*
淡路結び・*awaji-musubi*
Abalone knot

結婚の祝儀用に使われることの多い結び。両端を引っ張ると結びがより締まる。

This is a Josephine knot that is often used for weddings. When both ends are pulled, the knot tightens.

鮑返し・*awabi-gaeshi*
淡路返し・*awaji-gaeshi*
Ornate abalone knot

鮑（淡路）結びを応用したもの。長い水引を切ることなく結ぶことができる。「切る」という言葉は物や人との繋がりが切れることを連想させ、祝いの場にふさわしくない「忌み言葉」とされる。

This is a complicated version of *awabi-musubi*. The knot is made by using up one long strip of *mizuhiki*, without cutting the ends. The word "cut" is disliked and considered to be inappropriate for celebratory occasions, since it suggests cutting ties or relationships with people and objects.

大入袋 · *oiri-bukuro*

Large attendance envelope

芝居や相撲で客が大勢入った（大入）ときに、関係者に慰労と祝いの気持ち
で配るお金を入れる。

An *oiri-bukuro* is an envelope used for giving money to show gratitude to
the staff when a large number of audiences and spectators come for theatre
plays or sumo wrestling.

ポチ袋 · *pochi-bukuro*

Small envelope

お年玉などを入れる袋。関西弁で「ほんの少し」という意味の「ぽちっと」、
関東弁は「これっぽち」という言葉が語源とされる。

A *pochi-bukuro* is a small envelope used for giving money. For example, it
is used when adults give money to children on New Year's Day.

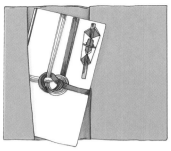

金封袱紗 · *kimpu-bukusa*
Gift cloth for money

台付き袱紗 · *daitsuki-fukusa*
Gift cloth with a board

袱紗 · *fukusa*

Gift cloth

贈答品は袱紗（ふくさ）や小風呂敷で包んで持参するのが本来だが、近年は持ち運びに便利な金封専用の袱紗がある。金封袱紗は二つ折りの布の内側に金封を挟む綴じがついたもの。台付き袱紗には塗り板が取り付けられており、その上に金封をのせて袱紗で包む。袱紗の包み方は祝儀と不祝儀で異なる。相手の目の前で袱紗を広げ、金封を渡すのがマナー。

Traditionally, gifts are wrapped in a *fukusa* or a *furoshiki* when carrying them from place to place. However, today, *fukusa* made specially for wrapping money to carry around are sold. One type has a pocket inside a twofold cloth. Another type has a lacquered board attached to the center of a square cloth so that the envelope with money inside can be set on this board and wrapped in cloth.

切手盆 · *kittebon*

Lacquered *kittebon* tray

祝儀袋や不祝儀袋（122頁）を相手に渡すときにのせる小ぶりな塗り盆。相手への進物を直接、手渡しすることは無礼とされていたために切手盆が正式であった。切手盆を持っていく際には袱紗に包んでおくのがマナー。

Since handing monetary gifts directly from hand to hand was considered to be impolite, this small tray called *kittebon* was used for placing the special envelopes for celebratory monetary gifts or those for monetary gifts offered as condolences (page 122).

神棚

神棚とは家の中に神社の神前を再現し、日々神様の召し上がり物を供えて礼拝する場所のこと。神社からいただいた御神札（おふだ）を祀（まつ）る。

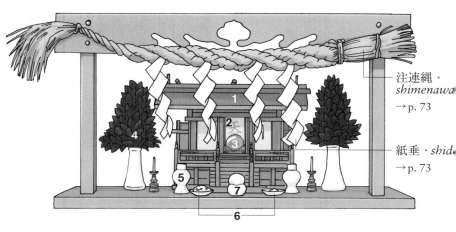

注連縄・*shimenawa*
→ p. 73

紙垂・*shid...*
→ p. 73

1

宮形・*miyagata*

Miniature shrine

神社を模した小形の社。一社造りや三社造りなどがある。イラストは「通し屋根三社造り」。

A *miyagata* is a miniature shrine for a household altar. It can have one door or three doors.

2

御神札（御札）・*ofuda*

Amulet

伊勢神宮内宮（ないくう）の御札（神宮大麻）を中心に、氏神様など崇拝する神社の御神札を祀って拝礼する。伊勢神宮内宮とは日本の神・天照大御神（あまてらすおおみかみ）が祀られている神社で、全国の神社の総鎮守。伊勢神宮の外宮や別宮にはほかの神が祭られている。

The *ofuda* from the Naiku of the Ise Jingu is placed at the center, together with others from local shrines. The Naiku of the Ise Jingu is a Shinto shrine dedicated to Amaterasu-Omikami, the god of all shrines in Japan.

A *kamidana* is an altar placed inside a household for enshrining the Shinto god. Food is offered every day, and an amulet from a shrine is placed on the altar.

3

神鏡・*shinkyo*

Sacred mirror

神社の神前では、鏡は神の御霊代（みたましろ）、依り代として中央に据えられている。この鏡を「神鏡」と呼ぶ。それにならい、神棚にも神鏡を置く。

A *shinkyo* is a mirror that is placed before god in shrines. This mirror is a place for god to dwell and it is also placed in household altars.

4

榊・*sakaki*

Cleyera japonica

ツバキ科の常緑小高木で、古くから神事に用いられるため「榊」という字をあてられている。榊は毎月1日と15日に取り替えるのがならわし。

This is an evergreen tree of the Theaceae family and is used for shrine rituals. Freshed *sakaki* branches are offered on the first and fifteenth of every month.

5

瓶子・*heishi*

Sacred sake bottles

御神酒（おみき）を入れて供える、左右一対の器。

Heishi is a pair of bottles for holding sacred sake.

6

平瓮・*hiraka*

Dish for sacred rice or salt

米と塩を入れて供える器。

A *hiraka* is a dish for offering rice and salt.

7

水玉・*mizutama*／水器・*suiki*

Water container

水を入れて毎日供える蓋付きの器。

A *mizutama* is a lidded container for offering water.

仏壇

仏壇は家の中に寺院の仏殿を再現し、仏像を祀り、先祖の霊を供養するための場所である。

A *butsudan* is a miniature Buddhist sanctum placed inside a household for the souls of ancestors on which a statue or an image of Buddha is placed.

仏壇 · *butsudan*

Buddhist family altar

本尊や位牌を安置するための箱状の祭壇。内部は寺院の内陣（本尊を祀る場所）を模しているため、仏壇の中心は位牌ではなく本尊である。位牌を本尊の近くに祀るのは、「亡くなった人はすべて仏になる」という仏教思想による。供え物は「香＝線香」「花」「灯燭（とうしょく）＝ロウソク」「浄水」「飲食（おんじき）＝ご飯」の「五供（ごくう）」が基本とされる。仏壇の構造や仏具、供え物は各宗派によって異なる。

A *butsudan* is a box altar for placing the statue of Buddha or a memorial plaque. The interior is made to resemble the area in a temple where the Buddhist statue is placed. Therefore the statue but not the memorial praque comes at the center of the altar. The plaque is placed by the statue due to the Buddhist concept that the deceased become a special existence close to Buddha.

___
1

本尊 · *honzon*

Main statue or image of Buddha

本尊とは、寺院に祀られている仏像の中で、最も中心となる仏像のこと。仏壇においては中に祀る仏像を「ご本尊」と呼ぶことが多い。本尊は宗派によって異なる。イラストのように、仏像が描かれた小さな掛け軸（99頁）を飾る場合もある。

The *honzon* is the most important statue or image of Buddha that is enshrined in a temple. The statue of Buddha enshrined in Buddhist family altars are often referred to as *gohonzon*. Different sects worship different Buddha. As shown in the picture, a small hanging scroll (page 99) with an image of Buddha can be hung.

___
2

位牌 · *ihai*

Memorial plaque

故人の仏名（戒名／かいみょう）を書いた木牌。裏には俗名と没年月日、享年が書かれる。朝晩、仏像と位牌を拝み、供養をして故人を偲（しの）ぶ。

An *ihai* is a wooden plaque with the alterlife name of the deceased. On the backside, the name, date of death and age at death are inscribed. Every morning and night, people pray before the statue of Buddha and the plaque to remember the dead.

火葬後の遺骨や骨壺は墓地に埋葬する。墓の形は地域によってさまざまだが、納骨室の上に台石と棹石を重ねた「和型墓石」が一般的。

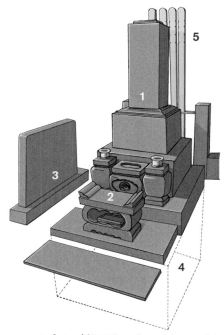

1

棹石 · *sao-ishi*／仏石 · *hotoke-ishi*

Gravestone

「○○家之墓」といった家名などの文字が刻まれる石。仏様を迎えるための石とされている。

A *sao-ishi* is a stone on which the family name is engraved. It is a stone for welcoming the spirits of ancestors.

2

香炉（墓前用） *kouro* (to place before a grave)

Incense burner

線香を供えるところ。イラストのように、石をくり抜いた中に線香を寝かせて供えるタイプのものは、風で火が消えにくく、上には経典や供え物が置けるようになっている。

A *kouro* is used for offering incense sticks. Some are made of stone inside which incense sticks are set so that the flames do not go out easily with the wind. Buddhist scriptures and offerings can be placed on top.

Graves

Ashes and urns are buried in graveyards. The style of graves is different according to each region. The most common type is built with a headstone on a footstone which are placed above a cinerarium.

___
3

墓誌 · *boshi*

Tombstone inscription

その墓に埋葬されている先祖全員の戒名、生年月日、没年月日などが刻まれている。

A *boshi* is a type of tombstone which has the afterlife names, birth dates and death dates of all the ancestors who have been buried in the same grave.

___
4

納骨室 · *nokotsushitsu* ／カロート · *karoto*

Burial chamber

台石の下に遺骨や骨壺を安置する小室。納骨室のタイプは2種類ある。人の骨は土に還るという考えから、納骨室の底を土のままにして、骨壺から遺骨を出して納めるタイプ。もう一つは、底をコンクリートにして、骨壺のまま納めるタイプ。

A *nokotsushitsu* is a small interment space under the tombstone for placing ashes and urns. There are two types: one is bare earth, in which bones are taken out of the urns when placed; the other is concrete, in which bones are put in urns before they are placed.

___
5

卒塔婆 · *sotoba*

Wooden *sotoba* slat

仏名、戒名（かいみょう）などを書いて墓の後ろに立てる細長い板。釈迦の遺骨を埋葬した上に立てられた塔「ストゥーパ」に由来する名前で、先端が塔の形になっている。お盆やお彼岸など先祖供養の際に、寺院や霊園に頼んで用意する。

A *sotoba* is a long piece of wooden board placed behind the tomb with Buddhist names or alterlife names written on it. The name *sotoba* comes from stupa, which is an architectural structure built where the bones of Buddha are buried. The topmost part is shaped like a tower.

日本建築
JAPANESE TRADITIONAL ARCHITECTURE

あ	荒波紋	Raging wave	63
	犬矢来	Protective screen	12
	入母屋造り	Combination roof	20
	囲炉裏	Fireside	27
	縁側	Veranda	17
	大戸口	Entrance for the family	23
	大棟	Main ridge	18
	鬼瓦	Ridge-end tile	19
	おみくじ	Fortune slip	75
	折上天井	Coved ceiling	41
か	鏡天井	Mirror ceiling	40
	掛込天井	Sloped ceiling	49
	春日灯籠	*kasuga-doro*	52
	片手桶	Single-handled bath bucket	43
	片流れ	Shed roof	21
	火灯口	Servant's entrance	49
	火灯（花頭）窓	Firelight window	39
	釜	Cooker	25
	竈（かまど）	Cooking stove	25
	鴨居	Lintel	33
	茅葺き屋根	Thatched roofs	22
	枯山水庭園	Dry landscape garden	61
	給仕口	Servant's entrance	49
	切妻造り	Gabled roof	20
	降棟	Descending ridge	18
	竈（くど）	Cooking stove	25
	沓脱石	Shoe-removing stone	17
	懸魚	Fish-shaped gable ornament	78
	化粧屋根裏	Sloped ceiling	49

建仁寺垣	*kenninji-gaki*	55
格子窓	Lattice window	39
格天井	Coffered ceiling	40
向拝柱	*Kohai* column	79
五右衛門風呂	Cauldron bath	44
小猿鉤	Wooden friction stopper	27
腰板壁	Wainscoting	13
腰壁	Wainscoting	13
腰張	Waist-high paper skirting	49
五重塔	Five-storied pagoda	81
琴柱（徽軫）灯籠	*kotoji-doro*	53
狛犬	Guardian dogs	72
賽銭箱	Offertory box	72
棹縁天井	Board and batten ceiling	41
砂紋	Raked gravel pattern / sand pattern	61
鞘の間	Sheath room	33
沢渡石	Stepping stone	59
三尊石	Triad stones	58
枝折戸	Wicket gate	51
敷居	Door sill	33
式台玄関	Entrance for guests	23
四脚門	Four-legged gate	76
自在鉤	Pot hook	27
獅子	Guardian dogs	72
下地窓	Exposed frame window	38
紙垂（四手）	Paper streamer	73
注連縄	Ritual Shinto rope	73
鯱（しゃち）	*Shachihoko* ornaments	65
鯱（しゃちほこ）	*Shachihoko* ornaments	65
障子	Paper sliding door	37
浄土式庭園	Pure land garden	56
神明造り	*Shimmei*-style	69
神明鳥居	*Shimmei*-style gateway	66
水盤舎	Hand-washing shelter	71
水紋	Water ripple	63
鈴	Bell	74
簾	Blinds	17
砂盛	Raked gravel mound	60
青海波紋	Blue ocean wave	62
関守石	Barrier stone	51
銭湯	Public bath	42
相輪	Metal pagoda decorations	81

さ

た	大社造り	*Taisha*-style	68
	三和土	Earth or mortar floored area	25
	畳	Tatami	31
	違い棚	Staggered shelf	35
	池泉回遊式庭園	Pond-stroll garden	57
	手水舎	Hand-washing shelter	71
	蹲踞	Washbasin set	50
	付書院	Built-in desk	35
	坪庭	Pocket garden	16
	妻	Gable end wall	19
	妻側	Gable end wall	19
	出格子	Lattice window	39
	出書院	Built-in desk	35
	点前座	Host's place	48
	天守	Castle tower	64
	天袋	Ceiling cabinet	35
	塔灯篭	*to-doro*	53
	通り庭	Open corridor	15
	床	Alcove	34
	床の間	Alcove	34
	床脇	Side alcove	35
	飛石	Stepping stones	51
	戸袋	Shutter box	23
	土間	Earth or mortar floored area	25
	土間庇	Pent roof for *doma*	47
	留め石	Barrier stone	51
	鳥衾	Ornamental roof tile	78
な	長屋	Row house	28
	流造り	*Nagare*-style	70
	長押	Frieze rail	33
	仁王像	Two Deva Kings	77
	躙口	Crawl-through entrance	47
	塗り残し窓	Exposed frame window	38
	野天風呂	Open-air bath	45
	暖簾	Curtain	15
は	萩垣	*hagi-gaki*	54
	ハシリ	Open corridor	15
	破風	Roof gable	22
	羽目板張り	Boarded wall	13
	柄杓	Ladle	71
	檜風呂	Cypress bath	44
	平側	Exterior wall	19

	風鐸	Wind bell	81
	袋戸棚	Ceiling cabinet	35
	襖	Opaque sliding door	36
	仏殿	Buddhist sanctum	78
	踏石	Shoe-removing stone	17
	風呂桶	Bath bucket	43
	文化住宅	Semi-Western style house	29
	へっつい	Cooking stove	25
	扁額	Nameplate	47
	ペンキ絵	Mural painting	42
	宝形（方形）造り	Square pyramidal roof	21
	宝鐸（ほうたく）	Wind bell	81
	宝鐸（ほうちゃく）	Wind bell	81
ま	舞良戸	Wooden door with horizontal slats	15
	招き造り	Saltbox roof	21
	明神鳥居	*Myojin*-style gateway	67
	虫籠窓	Finely latticed window	13
	武者窓	Warrior's window	38
や	櫓	Turret	65
	矢来垣	*yarai-gaki*	55
	雪見灯籠	*yukimi-doro*	52
	寄棟造り	Hip roof	20
	四つ目垣	*yotsume-gaki*	54
	与力窓	Slatted window	38
ら	欄間	Decorative transom	31
	流水紋	Flowing water	62
	連子窓	Barred window	39
	楼門	Tower gate	77
	炉畳	Sunken hearth tatami mat	49
	露天風呂	Open-air bath	45
わ	脇床	Side alcove	35

索引（五十音順）

生活道具
JAPANESE TRADITIONAL
EVERYDAY THINGS

あ	足元行灯	Foot lamp	100
	淡路返し	Ornate abalone knot	125
	淡路結び	Abalone knot	125
	鮑返し	Ornate abalone knot	125
	鮑結び	Abalone knot	125
	衣桁	Clothing rack	86
	位牌	Memorial plaque	131
	印鑑	Stamp	107
	印章	Stamp	107
	印泥	Inkpad	107
	印肉	Inkpad	107
	馬乗提灯	*umanori-chochin*	103
	大入袋	Large attendance envelope	126
	小田原提灯	*odawara-chochin*	103
	御神札（御札）	Amulet	128
	折り紙	Origami	111
	折据	Card wrapper	120
	折り熨斗	Dried abalone	123
	折本	Folded book	113
か	階段箪笥	Staircase chest	85
	書付	Box inscription	115
	掛け紙	*Noshi* wrapping paper for gifts	123
	掛け軸	Hanging scroll	99
	掛物	Hanging scroll	99
	飾り棚	Ornamental shelf	86
	勝手屏風	Screen for kitchen	97
	蚊取り線香	Mosquito coil	92
	蚊取り豚	Pig-shaped incense holder	92
	蚊帳	Mosquito net	91
	蚊遣り線香	Mosquito coil	92
	蚊遣り豚	Pig-shaped incense holder	92
	カロート	Burial chamber	133
	巻子	*Washi* scroll	112
	関東火鉢	Rectangular brazier	90
	聞香炉	Incense burner	119
	切手盆	Lacquered *kittebon* tray	127

	脇息	Armrest	89
	鏡台	Dressing table	87
	桐簞笥	Paulownia-wood chest of drawers	84
	銀葉	Silver sheet	119
	銀葉盤	Tray for *gin-yo*	121
	源氏香	The Genjiko chart	121
	源氏香之図	The Genjiko chart	121
	硯屏	Screen for inkstone	105
	香炭団	Charcoal	120
	香木	Aromatic tree	118
	行李	Wicker box	93
	香炉	Incense burner	119
	香炉（墓前用）	Incense burner	132
さ	座椅子	Legless chair	89
	棹石	Gravestone	132
	榊	Cleyera japonica	129
	座卓	Low table	88
	真田紐	*Sanada himo* cord	115
	座布団	Floor cushion	89
	桟蓋	Framed lid	117
	色紙	Paperboard	112
	自在	Adjusting hook	99
	祝儀袋	Special envelope for celebratory monetary gifts	122
	神鏡	Sacred mirror	129
	水器	Water container	129
	水滴	Dropper	106
	姿見	Full-length mirror	87
	硯	Inkstone	105
	墨	Ink	105
	卒塔婆	Wooden *sotoba* slat	133
た	炭団	Charcoal	120
	短檠	Short oil lamp	101
	短冊	Paper strip	112
	檀紙	High-grade *washi* paper	109
	卓袱台	Low dining table	88
	提灯	Paper lantern	102
	千代紙	*Chiyogami*	110
	衝立	Screen	95
	葛籠	Lacquered wicker box	93
	手焙り	Hand-warmer	90
	手燭	Portable candlestick	101

な	長火鉢	Rectangular brazier	90
	長持	Trunk	94
	練香	Solid perfume	118
	納骨室	Burial chamber	133
	熨斗	Dried abalone	123
	熨斗鮑	Dried abalone	123
	熨斗紙	*Noshi* wrapping paper for gifts	123
は	箱書	Box inscription	115
	箱簞笥	Staircase chest	85
	半紙	Half-sized *washi* paper	109
	筆架	Brush rest	105
	屏風	Folding screen	96
	平瓮	Dish for sacred rice or salt	129
	袱紗	Gift cloth	127
	不祝儀袋	Special envelope for monetary gifts as condolences	122
	仏壇	Buddhist family altar	131
	筆	Writing brush	104
	文鎮	Paperweight	106
	瓶子	Sacred sake bottles	129
	奉書紙	Ceremonial *washi* paper	109
	墓誌	Tombstone inscription	133
	ポチ袋	Small envelope	126
	仏石	Gravestone	132
	本尊	Main statue or image of Buddha	131
	盆提灯	*bon-chochin*	102
ま	祭り提灯	*matsuri-chochin*	102
	真結び	Square knot	124
	水玉	Water container	129
	水引	*Mizuhiki* cord	124
	水屋屏風	Screen for kitchen	97
	乱衣装箱	Clothing box	94
	乱箱	Clothing box	94
	宮形	Miniature shrine	128
	結び切り	Square knot	124
	毛筆	Writing brush	104
	両輪結び	Flower knot	124
や	四方掛け結び	Four-direction knot	115
ら	落成款識	Signature	117
	落款	Signature	117
わ	和紙	*Washi* paper	108
	和装本	Japanese-style book	113

| 和帳 | Japanese-style book | 113 |
| 和綴じ本 | Japanese-style book | 113 |

監 修	山本成一郎 （やまもと・せいいちろう）
	建築家。
	早稲田大学理工学研究科（大学院）建設工学修了。
	2001年に山本成一郎設計室を開設。

| イラスト | 末吉詠子 |

| 翻 訳 | 髙尾桃子 |

| 校 正 | Sally BALL |

| デザイン | 奥野正次郎（POROROCA） |

| Editorial Supervision | YAMAMOTO Seiichiro |

| Illustration | SUEYOSHI Eiko |

| Translation | TAKAO Toko |

| Proofing | Sally BALL |

| Design | OKUNO Shojiro（POROROCA） |

英訳付き ニッポンの名前図鑑　日本建築・生活道具

2018年2月20日　初版発行
2019年7月 8 日　３版発行

編　者　　　淡交社編集局
発行者　　　納屋嘉人
発行所　　　株式会社 淡交社
　　　　　　本社　〒603-8588京都市北区堀川通鞍馬口上ル
　　　　　　営業　075-432-5151　　編集　075-432-5161
　　　　　　支社　〒162-0061東京都新宿区市谷柳町39-1
　　　　　　営業　03-5269-7941　　編集　03-5269-1691
　　　　　　www.tankosha.co.jp

印刷・製本　　三晃印刷株式会社

©2018 淡交社　Printed in Japan
ISBN978-4-473-04237-8

An Illustrated Guide to Japanese Traditional Architecture and Everyday Things

This book was published in 2018
by Tankosha Publishing Co., Ltd.

シリーズ
英訳付き ニッポンの名前図鑑

和食・年中行事

An Illustrated Guide
to Japanese Cooking
and Annual Events

監修　服部幸應

蕎麦湯をつぐ"あの"容器は、
なんていう名前？
"門松"は英語で
どのように説明したらいい？

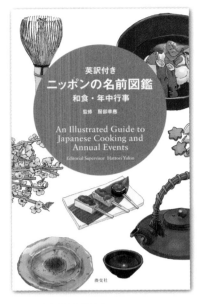

ISBN 978-4-473-04181-4
A5判変型 160頁　本体1,400円＋税

シリーズ
英訳付き ニッポンの名前図鑑

和服・伝統芸能

An Illustrated Guide
to Japanese Traditional Clothing
and Performing Arts

監修　市田ひろみ

結婚式でよく観る
"あの"黒い和服の名前は？
"しごき帯"って、
どんなもの？

ISBN　978-4-473-04195-1
A5判変型 160頁　本体1,400円＋税